School of Divinity

Gardner-Webb University
School of Divinity

PROVERBS
The Secret of
Beautiful Living

James T.

The Secret of

Draper, Jr.

ERBS

Beautiful Living

Tyndale House
Publishers, Inc.
Wheaton, Illinois

All Scriptures quoted in this book
are taken from *The Living Bible*
© 1971 by Tyndale House
Publishers, Wheaton,
Illinois, except those indicated
as being from the King James
Version (KJV).

Library of Congress Catalog
Card Number 76-58132. ISBN
0-8423-4925-1, cloth. Copyright ©
1977 by James T. Draper, Jr. All
rights reserved.
First printing, April 1977.
Printed in the United States of
America.

Dedicated to

RANDY, BAILEY, & TERRI

*my sons and daughter—
gifts of a gracious God
entrusted to me for the brief
years of their childhood to love,
encourage, direct, and guide
to the heavenly Father.
Their lives have been my greatest joy,
and the beautiful principles
of the book of Proverbs
have been winsomely evident
in their lives.*

CONTENTS

YEARS AGO Daddy got me in the habit of reading a chapter of Proverbs a day (thirty-one days in the usual month, thirty-one chapters of Proverbs).

It is a delightful, practical, inexhaustible source of sound common sense, enabling us, if we but apply it to our own lives faithfully, to put shoes on our faith.

RUTH BELL GRAHAM

INTRODUCTION

Many volumes have been written about theology and the academics of the Christian faith. Yet little has been written on the very practical admonitions found in Proverbs. In that delightful book, we are given wise counsel concerning how to live successfully on a day-to-day basis.

It was out of a deep sense of need that I personally began to study Proverbs. First, I tried to list the various areas of concern mentioned in the book. Then I endeavored to trace these ideas through the book. The volume you have in your hand is the outgrowth of that study. It is not a theological book. It is not concerned with the philosophy of religion or with apologetics. It is simply an attempt to get the teachings of Proverbs down to where we live, to make their application practical for our everyday lives.

I would suggest that you first take several hours and read Proverbs in a single sitting. The overall impact of the book will be important to you, and there is no better way to get that overview than to read the entire book at one time. Do not worry about retention of specific details; just let the Holy Spirit bring to you what he has in mind from such a reading. You will then be ready to pursue the study of this volume. Do it with an open Bible and trace the concepts throughout Proverbs as you read.

My prayers are with you as you begin this study.

1
The Beginning of Knowledge

In his Word, God provides us with precepts intended not merely to give us head knowledge, but also the skill to work out that knowledge in our lives. Each one of us ought to want to live beautifully and pleasingly before God. To do so brings pleasure to God and is the fulfillment of his purposes for our lives.

In the opening verses, the writer of Proverbs describes the foundation upon which such a life is to be built. "These are the proverbs of King Solomon of Israel, David's son: He wrote them to teach his people how to live—how to act in every circumstance, for he wanted them to be understanding, just and fair in everything they did. 'I want to make the simple-minded wise!' he said. 'I want to warn young men about some problems they will face. I want those already wise to become the wiser and become leaders by exploring the depths of meaning in these nuggets of truth' " (1:1-6).

Proverbs is filled with illustrations of divine truth put in such a way that we can appropriate and bring that truth into our lives and experiences. The style is not the bold confrontation of the preacher, but the subtle use of sayings and riddles that deal with the practical matters of life. The phrase translated "the depths of meaning" (l:6) simply means "riddles." A riddle is a saying that has to be interpreted because its meaning is not readily apparent. In Proverbs truth is presented to us in ways that make us think and reflect as it works its way into our hearts.

The key word throughout Proverbs is "wisdom." We find it in the opening passage of the book—"The fear of the Lord is the beginning of knowledge: but fools despise wisdom (Hebrew, *chokmah)* and instruction" (1:7, KJV). It is important at the very outset for us to define wisdom. It does not simply mean "knowledge" (Hebrew, *daath).* Compare 9:10: "The fear of the Lord is the beginning of wisdom (Hebrew, *chokmah)."*

In the Old Testament, "knowledge" means information or eternal truth. "Wisdom" refers to skill. If one is wise in knowing how to do something, he has skill in it. There is a difference between having knowledge in our head and wisdom in our lives. The mere bringing of divine knowledge and divine revelation into our minds is not enough. Such knowledge is intended to be worked out in our lives.

Take, for example, how God worked with his people as recorded in Exodus. God said to Moses, "Instruct those to whom I have given special skill as tailors to make the garments that will set him (Aaron) apart from others, so that he may minister to me in the priest's office" (Exodus 28:3). "Special skill" in this text is again the Hebrew word *chokmah,* "wisdom." God said that those tailors had been given wisdom so they were able to take a piece of material, dye it, and do all the things necessary to make a beautiful garment for the priest.

Later on the Book of Exodus declares, "All the other craftsmen with God-given abilities are to assist Bezalel and Oholiab in constructing and furnishing the Tabernacle" (36:1). The Hebrew word for wisdom is here called a God-given ability. It is some special skill designed to serve God in the work of the sanctuary.

God gives us wisdom to equip us, to enable us to live as we ought to live. Proverbs does not take us to church very often. Instead, it takes us to our businesses, our schools, our homes, and our personal relationships with others. The religion of our God is a way of life. It is something that we live every day, not something we reserve for the sanctuary. The message of Christianity is intended to be worked out in our lives. The Word of God is living truth that comes into our minds and hearts to be seen, to be expressed in the way we live.

The actual proverbs of Proverbs begin in the tenth chapter. The first nine chapters are exhortations, admonishing the reader to prepare himself to heed the sayings that follow. These chapters of exhortation often use the phrase "my son." Proverbs was evidently written by King Solomon to his son in order to equip him to be king. It was written to a young person. But older persons also need to give heed to its message because God has given to them the privilege of giving counsel, advising and encouraging young people to grow and mature in the Lord. Proverbs has application for us all.

The meaning and value of Proverbs is especially seen when we realize that we, too, are children of the King.

Jesus Christ has made us to be royalty (1 Peter 2:9). The book of Proverbs is God's Word to us, to help us know how sons of the King ought to live. There is great application, great blessing, and great meaning for all of us in this wonderful book.

REVERENCE

"The fear of the Lord is the beginning of knowledge" (1:7, KJV). Reverence is the first element needed to build a beautiful and pleasing life before God. "Fear of the Lord" does not signify fright, cowardice, or terror. It actually means "respect" and "reverence." In fact, *The Living Bible* translates it like this—"the first step is to trust and reverence the Lord!"

We are to come before God in awe because of who he is and what he does. When we compare ourselves with him, we find that we are sinful and he is holy. We are base and finite, but God is glorious and limitless. We come before God as sinners before a holy God. Because of his very being, we come to him in reverence, awe, and respect. To put it another way, the fear of the Lord means we are to come before God in worshipful submission. We are to bow our knees before him and commit our lives to him. That is the fear and reverence the Lord requires.

This reverence for God is pivotal in our lives. If we do not come to God in submission and reverence, we can never have the skill to experience life as it ought to be lived. We will be defeated by our circumstance. We will be overwhelmed by the tragedies that constantly force themselves upon us. We will be disappointed by the waning affection of friends and the misunderstandings of associates. Our lives will be clouded with despair unless we come before God in reverential, worshipful submission. When we do so come before him, we take the initial step toward gaining the wisdom, the skill we need to live beautifully and pleasingly before the Lord.

This tells us something about God. We are introduced to him by the word "Lord," a word appearing in Proverbs more than 100 times. The Hebrew word used here is transliterated "Yahweh," and can be translated "Jehovah" or "the Lord." It is the name God used with his people because of his covenant relationship with them. It identifies our God as One who reveals himself and promises us a future. It is the personal name for our God, and we are his children.

The writer of Proverbs believed that God is not merely an idea, an abstraction of thought, or an impersonal first cause of existence. Rather, he believed God to be a personal God who has a name. The God of Proverbs is indeed the God revealed throughout the entire Word of God. He is a personal God who longs for fellowship with men and women. We can call his name. We can meet him. We can enter into a relationship with him. We can commit our lives to him. He makes promises to us. Our whole purpose of life is to come to know God and to come into a relationship with him. The fear of the Lord is the starting point of that relationship.

We need to beware of God's becoming too commonplace to us. I shudder when I hear people talking about God as their "bosom buddy" or "dear friend."

He is everything a buddy will be, but he is infinitely more than that. He is a holy God. He is the God of eternity. We never come to him except through Jesus Christ. We never come to God until we bow our knees to him and bring our unrighteousness before him. Then he makes us righteous through the blood of Jesus Christ. Without that experience we can never approach God in reverence and respect. God forbid that we should ever lose our sense of awe as we come before him.

REALITY

A second element presented in our text is that of reality: "The fear of the Lord is the beginning of knowledge." We normally think of a beginning as something that happened at one point in time, then was left behind as we went on to something else. In this passage the word "beginning" has nothing to do with chronology. Instead it refers to a "starting point." It is the place where we begin, but it is more. It continues to be the controlling principle of our relationship with God. It is the very heart of life for us. We begin with the fear of God, and we never leave it behind. Everyday it continues to be at the center of our relationship with him. It is the beginning and the continuing impact of God upon our hearts.

There is no one on this earth more miserable than a carnal Christian. He has moved away from God and has lost that reverential awe that accompanied his conversion experience. We start our relationship with God by

bowing our knees before him and inviting him into our
hearts to be our Savior and Lord. That is to be the
continuing experience of our lives day by day. "The
just shall live by faith" (Romans 1:17, KJV). We who are
the children of God are to keep on living by faith. Reverential awe and submission is our beginning attitude,
but it is also to be the continuing core of our relationship with God. Every day we are to bow before him.
Every day we are to remain close to him, walk with
him, live with him, serve him.

That's God's design for our experience as his children. When we get away from that, we lose our closeness to God. If God isn't real to us, frustration and
sadness will be.

RELATIONSHIP

Knowledge is basically a relationship. It does not matter how much we know about God. *We must know God.*
That knowledge is to be experienced. It is to be brought
into our lives and lived out through us. Proverbs
teaches us about the kind of wisdom and knowledge
that brings us into a living and continual relationship
with God. It provides us with the skills we need to have
victory and confidence before the Lord.

The book of Proverbs has a twofold purpose, according to 1:2. It teaches us how to act in every circumstance
by giving us moral wisdom and mental or intellectual
maturity. Moral wisdom applies God's guides for living. Intellectual maturity gives us the perception to rec-

ognize words of understanding. Mental growth is a part of the spiritual process in our lives. We are to have moral wisdom, but we are to have intellectual acumen as well. The two go hand in hand.

We are "to know wisdom and instruction; to perceive the words of understanding; to receive the instruction of wisdom, justice, and judgment, and equity" (1:2, 3, KJV). Proverbs tells us that we are to find the way to spiritual and intellectual maturity through instruction, the "instruction of wisdom."

Sometimes we have the idea that instruction is merely giving directions. Perhaps this is why so many develop techniques, methods, or rituals as their way to live. They seem to say, "Go straight ahead. Now take a left. Now stop. Now go. Do this. Don't do that. Go here. Go there." But that is not what the word "instruction" means. "Instruction" means "discipline" or "training." It is something we can put into practice, so we can become the kind of persons God wants us to be. There is no simple or quick method of achieving that kind of instruction.

Throughout the book of Proverbs we will see how God despises the lazy person. God declares that a person who is lazy is useless, not spiritual, one who will make ridiculous excuses for not doing what he needs to do. God tells us that such a man is foolish. If we are going to grow and mature and be what God wants us to be, we must work at it. It takes discipline, training, instruction. Proverbs is designed to train us, discipline us, assist us in becoming spiritually mature. It provides precepts and principles which can control our sinfulness and our waywardness and point us in the proper direction for our lives.

That discipline is going to involve justice (righteousness), judgment, and equity (1:3). The word "justice" means "to come up to God's standard." It involves seeing God's ideal for our lives and meeting that standard. We thus accept his will on a personal level.

The word "judgment" should be translated "justice." It refers to social righteousness. In other words, we are to do right by each other. If we come up to God's standard in our personal righteousness, then we are going to have a right attitude toward each other. We will be kind to one another. We will be considerate and compassionate to one another. If there ever has been a day when God's people have needed this admonition, it is today. Much of the hurt and harm that comes into our lives as Christians is caused by other Christians. The book of Proverbs will help us get along with each other. It will help us be kind to one another, love one another, hurt with one another, and lift one another to the Father.

The word "equity" could be translated "integrity." It is concerned with fair play. It urges us to be honest with each other. If we are people of uprightness, we will be people of integrity. God wants us to face life under the discipline and the training of justice, judgment, and integrity. That is how we apply the fear of the Lord to our lives.

The book of Proverbs contrasts the foolish man and the wise man. In a nutshell the difference is this: the fool never has time to listen to anyone. To the fool all knowledge dwells in him. He is right, the world is wrong, and that is all he needs to know.

But a wise man will listen and so increase his knowledge. He sharpens his skills. He realizes that we never arrive, never exhaust our potential to learn. We may say, "I have done all I can do." But God still longs to do more through us. That's why we read, "I want those already wise to become the wiser and become leaders by exploring the depths of meaning in these nuggets of truth" (1:5, 6). God wants us to know that our potential is unlimited. What God proposes to do with us only awaits our willingness to do it. If we are wise we will listen, we will hear, we will increase our knowledge and understanding of God's purposes in our lives.

That is what the book of Proverbs is about. It is to instruct us. It is to equip us to live. It is to teach us, train us, and discipline us in our attitudes toward life in a world that is antagonistic and hostile. Jesus himself said, "Don't imagine that I came to bring peace to the earth! No, rather, a sword" (Matthew 10:34). Wherever the gospel is preached, some will believe and some will be bitterly antagonistic. That will always be so. In a world like that, how are we to live? What are we to do with the discipline, the tragedies, and the opportunities of life? The book of Proverbs does not propose to change society. It proposes to give God's children the tools by which they can live within the framework of a disenchanted and hostile environment. If we will listen, we will learn. God will give us the skill to experience all of life in a beautiful, victorious way. That is what Proverbs is endeavoring to say.

An illustration of the intent of Proverbs can be seen in the life of Joseph, one of the twelve sons of Jacob. His father's favorite son, he was an arrogant child. He told his family about dreams he had in which he was obeyed and worshiped by the rest of the family. When asked if he meant that he would rule over them he would say, "Absolutely." He was obnoxious. This brash young upstart deserved all the hostility he got because of the kind of person he was. His brothers despised and hated him. One day they got an idea— "Let's kill him." After they threw him down into a pit, they had second thoughts. Reason won out and they decided not to kill him, but to sell him. They sold him to a caravan on its way to Egypt.

The obnoxious, arrogant young man was despised and detested by all. Only his father loved him. But something happened during the years before his family saw him again. He had been disciplined and brought under the power of the Word of God. He was a changed person. He had gained the wisdom, the equipment to live pleasingly before God. One of the most beautiful pictures in the Word of God shows Joseph, the prime minister of Egypt, as he reveals himself in compassion and love to his brothers. He was no longer arrogant and obnoxious. He was compassionate, loving, concerned. He saved them from starvation and brought them under his protection. That happened because he was a man who learned the skills of living. God had worked a miracle in his life.

That is conversion. It is an illustration of what God does in a heart. Whatever our past may have been, God can take our lives and rebuild them. When we bow our knees to the purposes of God, he will replace our ugliness and despair with beauty and strength. He will teach us to live as victors. He can give us a life that bears the indelible mark of his wisdom, a life of optimism, conquest, happiness, usefulness.

The fear of the Lord is the beginning of knowledge, of wisdom. That is the starting point. Fools despise wisdom and instruction. We must choose either to live in the power of God, under the discipline of his Word, or to live foolishly. The world offers no hope, no solution, no encouragement. God says, "I want you to have wisdom, the skill to experience life as it ought to be experienced." The choice is up to us.

The Essence of Wisdom

Wisdom is the skill to live in a way that is pleasing to God. It is not simply information in our heads. It is information that we put to use—where we live, where we work, and where we play.

"For the value of wisdom is far above rubies; nothing can be compared with it" (8:11). Nothing else the human heart desires can be compared with wisdom. Wisdom is not stagnant. It is not bound by tradition. It is creative. "Wisdom and good judgment live together, for wisdom knows where to discover knowledge and understanding. If anyone respects and fears God, he will hate evil. For wisdom hates pride, arrogance, corruption and deceit of every kind. I, Wisdom, give good advice and common sense. Because of my strength, kings reign in power. I show the judges who is right and who is wrong. Rulers rule well with my help. I love all who love me. Those who search for me shall surely find me. Unending riches, honor, justice and righteousness are mine to distribute. My gifts are better than the purest gold or sterling silver! My paths are those of justice and right" (8:12-20). What makes this wisdom more valuable than anything else in the world?

DISCIPLINE

Wisdom does not come to the undisciplined or the careless. It does not come with the casual application of knowledge. Wisdom is the product of careful and disciplined training in a person's life and heart. It calls for hard work. It is not accidentally obtained. It is a pursuit. It is a search.

"I walked by the field of a certain lazy fellow and saw that it was overgrown with thorns, and covered with weeds; and its walls were broken down. Then, as I looked, I learned this lesson:

> *'A little extra sleep,*
> *A little more slumber.*
> *A little folding of the hands to rest'*

means that poverty will break in upon you..." (24:30-34). The writer came by the vineyard of a lazy man. He saw that the weeds had taken over the vineyard and the wall was broken down. He said, "I heed the warning. I looked at it and I was instructed. I looked at it and I listened. I learned."

A vital part of discipline involves heeding the warnings God gives from the experiences of life and from the pages of his Word. Letting God instruct and warn us is a part of the discipline that comes with God's wisdom working in our lives.

Another feature of discipline is correction or chastening. "Young man, do not resent it when God chastens and corrects you, for his punishment is proof of his love. Just as a father punishes a son he delights in to make him better, so the Lord corrects you" (3:11, 12). The chastening of God is comparable to our own family discipline. When our children need correction, we discipline them. Sometimes that means we must spank or punish them. As they grow older we may need to restrict them in some other way. God does the same thing with us. When we step away from God's blueprint, we are disciplined.

"And have you quite forgotten the encouraging words God spoke to you, his child? He said, 'My son, don't be angry when the Lord punishes you. Don't be discouraged when he has to show you where you are wrong. For when he punishes you, it proves that he loves you. When he whips you, it proves you are really his child.' Let God train you, for he is doing what any loving father does for his children. Whoever heard of a son who was never corrected? If God doesn't punish you when you need it, as other fathers punish their sons, then it means that you aren't really God's son at all—that you don't really belong in his family. Since we respect our fathers here on earth, though they punish us, should we not all the more cheerfully submit to God's training so that we can begin really to live? Our earthly fathers trained us for a few brief years, doing the best for us that they knew how, but God's correction is always right and for our best good, that we may share his holiness. Being punished isn't enjoyable while it is happening—it hurts! But afterward we can see the result, a quiet growth in grace and character" (Hebrews 12:5-11). Chastening is a part of discipline.

We have a tendency to think that "chastening" in the Word of God always means "punishment." Not so. Actually it means "training." Chastening is the way God trains us through the practical experiences of life. It is the way God leads us. It is the way God smooths and polishes our rough edges in order to equip us and prepare us to be well-fitted stones in the building of the household of God. That is an essential part of discipline.

Reproof is part of discipline too. God says, "Come here and listen to me! I'll pour out the spirit of wisdom upon you, and make you wise" (1:23). Reproof is God's dealing with us when we have deviated from his basic principles for our lives.

When we experience God's discipline, we will gain the wisdom to use our time wisely. One of the greatest sins that God's people commit in our affluent society is that we waste time. We spend our energies on pursuits that have little value or lasting import. Discipline helps us use our days well. "Wisdom gives: A long, good life, riches, honor, pleasure, peace" (3:16). "Teach us to number our days and recognize how few they are; help us to spend them as we should" (Psalm 90:12). When we are disciplined in the wisdom of God, we learn to spend our time wisely.

Wisdom also helps us learn to communicate properly. "From a wise mind comes careful and persuasive speech" (16:23). Each one of us needs to achieve such a level of communication. How different we would be if we could eliminate the unnecessary, sarcastic, and divisive speech that unsettles our contact with God and alienates us from our Christian brethren. Discipline is a needed part of our lives as we pursue wisdom.

When we have a disciplined life we also find happiness. "Young man, do not resent it when God chastens and corrects you, for his punishment is proof of his love. Just as a father punishes a son he delights in to make him better, so the Lord corrects you" (3:11). If we want to be happy, we must let our lives be disciplined by the wisdom of God. We will find happiness only when we live by his principles. We will find wealth too: "For such wisdom is far more valuable than precious jewels. Nothing else compares with it" (3:14, 15). Real wealth and genuine riches come from the wisdom of God.

UNDERSTANDING

The word "understanding," used frequently in Proverbs, comes from a root word which means "to discern," and is very closely related to the preposition "between." In 1 Kings 3:9 Solomon prayed for the ability to discern between good and evil. That is the concept of understanding.

Understanding simply means to see things as God sees them and to identify things the way God identifies them. "I, Wisdom, give good advice and common sense. Because of my strength, kings reign in power" (8:14). There is strength in understanding, a part of wisdom. The wise man has understanding with discretion; he sees things as they really are. An illustration of this is found in 6:32: "But the man who commits adultery is an utter fool, for he destroys his own soul." If we see things from God's vantage point, we know that immorality is the most damaging thing we can do with our lives. It will destroy us. We do not have the discretion to know this unless we have wisdom. If we have understanding, we actually see life situations through God's eyes.

Understanding (and its cousin, common sense) is emphasized throughout the book of Proverbs. For example, "Men with common sense are admired as counselors; those without it are beaten as servants" (10:13). "And, 'Learn to be wise,' he said, 'and develop good judgment and common sense! I cannot overemphasize this point.' Cling to wisdom—she will protect you. Love her—she will guard you! And with your wisdom, develop common sense and good judgment" (4:5-7). "Everyone admires a man with good sense, but a man with a warped mind is despised" (12:8). "For the Lord grants wisdom! His every word is a treasure of knowledge and understanding. He grants good sense to the godly—his saints. He is their shield, protecting them and guarding their pathway" (2:6-8). "A wise youth makes hay while the sun shines, but what a shame to see a lad who sleeps away his hour of opportunity" (10:5). Any farm hand with common sense knows he cannot sleep through a harvest. Too many things can destroy a crop if it is not gathered at the right time.

Some people have a lot of head knowledge but no

common sense. They know a lot but can't apply their knowledge to life. We cannot live properly without common sense. Wisdom is the skill to live a beautiful life. It is the application of knowledge. Wisdom is common sense at work in everyday relationships.

SHREWDNESS

The word "shrewdness" sometimes carries with it a bad connotation. A shrewd man is often thought of as being evil, or crafty, or taking advantage of others. But the word "shrewd" literally describes a person who looks around, sizes up a situation, and knows what is going on in it. He is aware of what is happening. He sees life in the perspective of its opportunities.

We see this in the following verses: "These are the proverbs of King Solomon of Israel, David's son: He wrote them to teach his people how to live—how to act in every circumstance, for he wanted them to be understanding, just and fair in everything they did. 'I want to make the simple-minded wise!' he said. 'I want to warn young men about some problems they will face. I want those already wise to become the wiser and become leaders by exploring the depths of meaning in these nuggets of truth' " (1:1-6).

The writer of Proverbs wants us to become shrewd about the issues of life and thus avoid pitfalls that would trip us in our pursuit of happiness. He wants us to know what life is all about. He wants us to know the dangers ahead so we can avoid them. This shrewdness is part of the wisdom that God wants to give us.

How sad it is when we fall victim to the same traps our parents did. We haven't learned from their mistakes. Similarly, we can look at history and see general patterns about the rise and fall of civilization. There is no possibility of American civilization surviving unless we learn from the past. We will not be aware of the details that would make us shrewd about life.

God says, "I want to help you chart your course through the uncharted seas that lie ahead of you. I want to give you shrewdness and understanding. I want to give you my wisdom."

That is what we read in Proverbs: "For wisdom and truth will enter the very center of your being, filling your life with joy. You will be given the sense to stay away from evil men who want you to be their partners in crime" (2:10, 11). Elsewhere we read, "A prudent man foresees the difficulties ahead and prepares for them; the simpleton goes blindly on and suffers the consequences" (22:3). Unless we allow the wisdom of God to pervade our minds and control our hearts, to give us a shrewdness, a discretion, an understanding of all that stretches before us, we shall fall into the same pitfalls that overthrew those who walked before us. God wants us to avoid those disasters.

DOCTRINE

There is one other ingredient of the wisdom God describes to us in the book of Proverbs—doctrine. We could also call it "knowledge" or "learning." A wise man knows the truth. More than that, he knows God. In fact, if we do not know God, we cannot know the truth. Jesus said, "I am the Way—yes, and the Truth and the Life. No one can get to the Father except by means of me" (John 14:6).

The essence of wisdom is full knowledge, complete doctrine—not only knowledge of the facts, but a knowledge of God himself. "You will soon learn the importance of reverence for the Lord and of trusting him" (2:5). "Don't ever trust yourself. In everything you do, put God first, and he will direct you and crown your efforts with success" (3:5, 6). An awareness and understanding of God leads us to a commitment to him. This is a part of the wisdom God wants us to know and experience.

"For the reverence and fear of God are basic to all wisdom. Knowing God results in every other kind of understanding" (9:10). In this passage "knowing" means "to know by experience." The wise man knows God, and the essence of wisdom is wrapped up in God. God is the beginning and the end of wisdom. He is the One who brings discipline into our lives. He is the One who gives us understanding and common sense. He brings shrewdness into our lives, as well as knowledge and learning. Wisdom begins, ends, and finds its full expression in God.

To the writer of Proverbs, the wise man is one who completely trusts in God. We are not to be wise in our own sight. We are to stay away from evil, choosing rather to acknowledge God in all of our ways.

All of this brings us to the point of our commitment

to God. Many today have a lot of knowledge about the Bible, but do not seem to know very much about God. They know what the Bible says, but don't know how to put it into practice. They seem to be unaware of God's presence in their lives, or of the reality of his Spirit within them. Such persons are often depressed, defeated, discouraged. They have knowledge, but they lack the skills needed to live a life that pleases God.

There was a halfway house in the Swiss Alps where travelers and mountain climbers could stop and rest before proceeding to the mountain summit. A crippled man worked at that halfway house. He always watched the travelers as they came and went. He watched as some sat in exhaustion and watched the others climb on to the summit. He would watch the disappointment come into their eyes as they realized they had missed the joy of successful adventure. He also saw those who had traveled to the summit and now were on their way back down. He saw the happiness in their eyes as they expressed the thrill of what they had seen. He wanted to go to the top of that mountain more than anything else in the world. But he was crippled. He could not do it.

One day a skilled guide said to him, "I will take you to the top." The cripple said, "But I cannot carry a pack. I cannot walk. My footsteps are too uncertain." The guide said, "I will help you. I will take you. Be ready in the morning. We will go to the top together." The crippled man spent a sleepless night. He was ready to go long before the appointed time. At last they set out on their journey. It was a tedious task. There were many places where the path was very narrow, and the guide had to hold the hand of the crippled man. There were places where the guide had to steady the man's foot. After considerable time and effort they stood on the summit. The cripple stood as tall as he could. He looked around and drank in the beauty, the awesomeness of the sight. Then he turned and fell on his knees before the guide and cried, "Sir, if it had not been for you, I would never have made it."

Someday we will stand on the summit of eternity, before the throne of our God. Those of us who know God will bow before him and declare, "God, if it had not been for you, I would never have made it." If we are going to make it, if we are going to know life, if we are going to walk wisely through time toward eternity, we must have the help of God. As we obey him and trust him, God will make us wise. He will enable us to live a beautiful and pleasing life before him.

The Demands of Wisdom

3

Wisdom is far more than the mere gathering of information. A person may have a great deal of information and not have wisdom. The book of Proverbs shows us how to take the wisdom and knowledge of eternity and put it into practice. That wisdom takes us out to where we live, work, and play. It speaks to us as we go about daily tasks and engage in our personal relationships. It helps us to react to those around us in the experiences of life. It enables us to understand life. That is the wisdom that God wants us to experience.

Wisdom never comes to the lazy, careless, or casual person. It is a pursuit that calls for diligent energy to be expended. It calls for persistence of effort. If we are going to be wise, something will be required of us. We must make a genuine commitment to God if we want to experience his wisdom in our lives.

Prerequisites for experiencing God's wisdom in our lives.

1. LISTENING TO GOD

There are three prerequisites for this kind of wisdom. First, we must have an attentive ear. If we would be wise, we must listen to God. Our Lord says, "I want those already wise to become the wiser and become leaders by exploring the depths of meaning in these nuggets of truth" (1:5).

The wise man listens with his heart as well as his ears. Jesus continually spoke of people who had ears to hear but did not hear. If we want wisdom, if we want to live skillfully, with fulfillment, purpose, direction, and satisfaction, we must listen to God. "For the reverence and fear of God are basic to all wisdom. Knowing God results in every other kind of understanding" (9:10).

"For the Lord grants wisdom! His every word is a treasure of knowledge and understanding"(2:6). We must listen to what God says if we are to experience his wisdom. All of the good information in the world will do us no good unless we hear and heed it. It matters not how sound the counsel or how good the advice if we do not listen to it. God's every word is rich with understanding. If we are going to gain wisdom, we must listen to him.

Wisdom comes from God; we cannot find it anywhere else. We cannot find wisdom in others. If we look for wisdom in our own imaginations and in our own thoughts, we will not find it. We must look to God for it.

The wise man takes God seriously. The wise man listens to the words of God. "Yes, if you want better insight and discernment, and are searching for them as you would for lost money or hidden treasure, then wisdom will be given you, and knowledge of God himself; you will soon learn the importance of reverence for the

Lord and of trusting him. For the Lord grants wisdom! His every word is a treasure of knowledge and understanding" (2:3-6).

God's words are trustworthy. "Every word of God proves true. He defends all who come to him for protection. Do not add to his words, lest he rebuke you, and you be found a liar" (30:5, 6). "The Lord's promise is sure. He speaks no careless word; all he says is purest truth, like silver seven times refined" (Psalm 12:6). We know that when God says something, we can believe it. We can trust in it. There is no need for misgivings about the Word of God. God means what he says and he says what he means.

A "great" theologian stood at a Baptist seminary recently and actually claimed that it is blasphemy to say that God has spoken through a completed Word. He said that restricts God and cuts down any possibility that God might have some revelation for us today. But God said all he wanted to say in his Word. He said it, he meant it, and that sealed it.

If we are going to be wise, we will not lean upon our own understanding, but will lean upon the wisdom of God. A man who disregards what God has to say is a fool. "Wisdom shouts in the streets for a hearing. She calls out to the crowds along Main Street, and to the judges in their courts, and to everyone in all the land: 'You simpletons!' she cries. 'How long will you go on being fools? How long will you scoff at wisdom and fight the facts? Come here and listen to me! I'll pour out the spirit of wisdom upon you and make you wise' " (1:20-23).

"How does a man become wise? The first step is to trust and reverence the Lord!" (1:7). If we want the kind of wisdom that enables us to be a blessing to those around us, we must trust God. And that involves listening to him.

2. TURNING FROM EVIL

A second demand of us if we are to experience God's wisdom is to turn from evil. "Come you simple ones without good judgment.... Leave behind your foolishness and begin to live; learn how to be wise" (9:4-6). This is the way to understanding. "Let him turn in hither: as for him that wanteth understanding, she saith to him, come, eat of my bread" (9:4, 5, KJV). Whoever wants understanding must turn from folly.

If we are to turn from evil, we must repent. "Turn in hither ... forsake the foolish, and live" (9:4, 6, KJV). The Scriptures stress repentance, which simply means to change direction. No man repents if he keeps the same attitude about things, if his life shows no change. Repentance is a reorientation of thought, a turning around and going the other way. Repentance causes us to forsake evil and to seek good. We cannot have wisdom without repentance.

"Wisdom shouts in the streets for a hearing.... 'You simpletons!' she cries. 'How long will you go on being fools? How long will you scoff at wisdom and fight the facts?' " (1:20, 22). When a man violates God's principles, when he goes on in his ignorance and rebellion, God admonishes him to turn. "Don't be conceited, sure of your own wisdom. Instead, trust and reverence the Lord, and turn your back on evil; when you do that, then you will be given renewed health and vitality (3:7, 8). "If anyone respects and fears God, he will hate evil. For wisdom hates pride, arrogance, corruption and deceit of every kind" (8:13). That is repentance. Though we once loved evil, now we hate it. Previously we turned away from God; now we turn to him.

After we repent in our hearts, then we confess our sins. We admit our sins, our failures to God. "A man who refuses to admit his mistakes can never be successful. But if he confesses and forsakes them, he gets another chance" (28:13). Confession is not telling God something he doesn't know. Rather we agree with God about ourselves. God declares that we are sinners. In our confession we say, "God, that's right. I admit it." We acknowledge our sins. We face up to our attitudes. We confess those things in us that are against God.

In the confession of his sinful involvement with Bathsheba, King David cried, "Oh, wash me, cleanse me from this guilt. Let me be pure again. For I admit my shameful deed—it haunts me day and night. It is against you and you alone I sinned, and did this terrible thing. You saw it all, and your sentence against me is just" (Psalm 51:2-4). Notice that he was specific about the sin he had committed. When we come to God, we are to acknowledge our transgressions to God and be specific in doing it. Confession of sin is a privilege, based on the invitation of God. "Seek the Lord while you can find him. Call upon him now while he is near. Let men cast off their wicked deeds; let them banish from their minds the very thought of doing wrong! Let them turn to the Lord that he may have mercy upon them, and to our God, for he will abundantly pardon!'' (Isaiah 55:6, 7).

Repentance and confession are hard for us, but the third part of turning from evil is beautiful. It is forgiveness. "He will abundantly pardon," said the prophet Isaiah. When we repent and confess, God forgives. In Proverbs 28:13 we saw that God's pardon gives us another chance. Through repentance, we come into contact with the loving heart of God. God longs to give mercy. He does not delight in judgment. The Son of God did not come into the world to condemn the world, but to redeem it. Hell becomes a human reality only because men refuse God's offer of holiness. But God is so serious about redeeming us that he gave his Son to die so that we could have forgiveness and salvation. That is God's desire.

The Psalmist tells us what happens when we confess our sins. "Oh, how great is your goodness to those who publicly declare that you will rescue them. For you have stored up great blessings for those who trust and reverence you. Hide your loved ones in the shelter of your presence, safe beneath your hand, safe from all conspiring men. Blessed is the Lord, for he has shown me that his never-failing love protects me like the walls of a fort!" (Psalm 31:19-21). "Lord, you have poured out amazing blessings on this land! You have restored the fortunes of Israel, and forgiven the sins of your people—yes, covered over each one" (Psalm 85:1, 2). "He is merciful and tender toward those who don't deserve it; he is slow to get angry and full of kindness and love. He never bears a grudge, nor remains angry forever. He has not punished us as we deserve for all our sins, for his mercy toward those who fear and honor him is as great as the height of the heavens above the earth. He has removed our sins as far away from us as the east is from the west" (Psalm 103:8-12).

3 · PERSISTING IN DEVOTION

"Happy is the man who is so anxious to be with me [Wisdom] that he watches for me daily at my gates, or waits for me outside my home!" (8:34). It is not enough for us to listen to God one time and then stop, or to merely begin a relationship with God. We must persist in devotion if we are going to have wisdom. That does not mean that we have to follow a certain life-style in order to keep our salvation. God will not go back on our forgiveness. But he does want us to walk wisely and winsomely. If we are going to experience victory, we must follow him daily.

"Every young man who listens to me and obeys my instructions will be given wisdom and good sense. Yes, if you want better insight and discernment, and are searching for them as you would for lost money or hidden treasure, then wisdom will be given you, and knowledge of God himself; you will soon learn the importance of reverence for the Lord and of trusting him" (2:1-5). God not only wants us to be saved, but he also wants us to deepen in our devotion. He doesn't seek an isolated act of repentance, but a lifetime of fellowship with him. This is a disciplined, persistent quest after discipleship. That is why Christians should be baptized, get into a Bible study, become involved in serving God. Then God can apply the great wisdom of eternity, revealed in his Word, to our hearts. We must continue walking with God if we are to allow God's wisdom to work in our daily experiences of life.

If we do not give ourselves to God, we will give ourselves to evil. We all give ourselves to something. "Don't you realize that you can choose your own master? You can choose sin (with death) or else obedience (with acquittal). The one to whom you offer yourself—he will take you and be your master and you will be his slave. Thank God that though you once chose to be slaves of sin, now you have obeyed with all your heart the teaching to which God has committed you. And now you are free from your old master, sin; and you have become slaves to your new master, righteousness. I speak this way, using the illustration of slaves and masters, because it is easy to understand: just as you used to be slaves to all kinds of sin, so now you must let yourselves be slaves to all that is right and holy" (Romans 6:16-19).

We must determine to be loyal to God. "And so, dear brothers, I plead with you to give your bodies to God. Let them be a living sacrifice, holy—the kind he can accept. When you think of what he has done for you, is this too much to ask? Don't copy the behavior and customs of this world, but be a new and different person with a fresh newness in all you do and think. Then you will learn from your own experience how his ways will really satisfy you" (Romans 12:1, 2).

If we are to have God's eternal wisdom, we must listen to him, turn from evil, and persist in our devotion to him.

The Things God Hates

Proverbs 6:16 tells us that "the Lord hates." That is very strong language. We know that God is capable of wrath, discipline, chastisement, but hatred? He is the eternal God of perfection, the Creator of the universe. Yet the writer of Proverbs dares to claim that there are some things God hates, that some things are an abomination to God.

Why does God hate these things? Because of what they do to us. Because of what happens when they enter the lives of his children. The heart of God hurts when there is a perversion of what he intended for man. When man experiences what God did not plan for him, it hurts God. It is an agony to him. Therefore he hates it. "For there are six things the Lord hates—no, seven: Haughtiness, lying, murdering, plotting evil, eagerness to do wrong, a false witness, sowing discord among brothers" (6:16-19).

WHAT GOD HATES
Notice the scope of the things God hates. It is all aimed at man. First, God hates haughtiness. This refers to the

manner in which we carry ourselves, the proud or pompous look. Next our tongues are brought into the picture—speaking falsely. Then God mentions wrong actions—murdering. Our reasoning process isn't blameless either—we plot evil. In fact, we have a basic disposition ("eagerness") to do wrong. Being "a false witness" is seen in many ways, even our habit of putting our best foot forward around those we seek to impress. We exaggerate our good and others' bad and so stir up discord among our associates.

This inclusive list warns us of the things we see, say, do, think, and love—and reveals the motives behind our actions.

Each of these sin types represents a perversion of its original intent. God never intended, for instance, for us to be proud or haughty, or for our tongues to lie. We pervert God's original purpose for us.

Several years ago I saw a movie on the life of Grover Cleveland Alexander, one of the greatest pitchers who ever threw a baseball. As I watched, I was so captivated that I found myself entering into the story. Little by little, I watched this superstar become a slave to alcohol. After he was released from his baseball team, he began to wander around the country, finally ending up in a circus sideshow. There he would stand on a platform to answer questions and talk about baseball. He was usually drunk while he did it. His viewers laughed at him and made fun of him. As I watched I felt as if I were there. Tears began to run down my cheeks. I clenched my fists and said, "Stop it! Stop it! He wasn't intended to be a freak in a sideshow! He was intended to throw a baseball better than anyone else who ever lived. That's what he was supposed to be. Not this!" His purpose in life had been perverted.

In that moment I realized something of the way God must feel when he looks down on his creation. He made man to have fellowship with him. Man was intended to love God with all his heart, to speak a word of witness for God, to declare eternal truth, to use his hands and feet to perform deeds of mercy and love, to share the grace of God. But his purpose is being perverted. His heart was never meant for evil and wickedness. His hands and his eyes were not intended to be perverted and prostituted by evil and wicked men. God never wanted it to be so. That is why God hates these things.

RESULTS OF THE THINGS GOD HATES

God hates haughtiness, "a proud look" (KJV). This indicates arrogance, disdain, swelling pride that views everyone else as inferior. This is doubtless listed first because pride is the basis of all other sins. It is pride that causes man to turn away from God. Pride is the beginning of rebellion, and the basis of disobedience.

If pride is left unharnessed in our hearts, we are playing into Satan's hands. The proud man says, "Let me tell you something, God. I can help you direct your universe." "But who can rebuke God, the supreme Judge?" (Job 21:22). The proud man boasts that he doesn't need God, but God will judge him. God describes his own actions by saying, "Give vent to your anger. Let it overflow against the proud. Humiliate the haughty with a glance; tread down the wicked where they stand" (Job 40:11, 12).

In the Bible the proud and the wicked are synonymous, but God's children are not to be so identified. We are to be subject one to another and clothed with humility because "God gives special blessings to those who are humble, but sets himself against those who are proud" (1 Peter 5:5). We will not have God's power when we need it if we harbor pride in our hearts. Uncontrolled and unrestrained pride destroys the vessel that contains it. God detests the self-sufficient and self-righteous look.

Some of us have the idea that it is easier for God to love us than it is for him to love somebody else. That's haughtiness, a proud look, a pharisaical look, self-righteousness. God knows that we are all sinners. We all stand equal before him. All men stand condemned in God's sight and need the grace of God. God hates haughtiness.

God also hates lying. In fact, this sin is listed twice. This first reference is to personal dishonesty and betrayal. Later in our text we will see the broader implications of perjury in a court of law.

"Truth stands the test of time; lies are soon exposed. Deceit fills hearts that are plotting for evil; joy fills hearts that are planning for good! No real harm befalls the good, but there is constant trouble for the wicked. God delights in those who keep their promises, and abhors those who don't" (12:19-22). If we lie, we will be caught. Since our lips were created to bring praise to

God, this is a perversion of God's intention for our lives. That is why God despises the lying tongue.

"You will destroy them for their lies; how you abhor all murder and deception" (Psalm 5:6). "Deliver me, O Lord, from liars. O lying tongue, what shall be your fate? You shall be pierced with sharp arrows and burned with glowing coals" (Psalm 120:2-4). "Hear the word of the Lord, O people of Israel. The Lord has filed a lawsuit against you listing the following charges: There is no faithfulness, no kindness, no knowledge of God in your land. You swear and lie and kill and steal and commit adultery. There is violence everywhere, with one murder after another" (Hosea 4:1, 2). In Revelation 21:8 we read that liars are among those who will be cast into the lake of fire. God wants his people to have personal honesty and integrity.

Lying is even a problem in the church of Jesus Christ. This involves much more than the things we say. There are many ways we imply things that are not true—by a glance, or by what appears to be an honest, simple question. God hates this. The list of broken hearts, broken homes, and broken churches that lie upon the rubbish heap of society because of lying tongues is tragic. It is little wonder that God despises lying. God forbid that we should ever give in to the temptation to misrepresent the truth.

Next we are told that God hates "murdering." This refers to a cruel disposition that will go to any length to get its way, even killing. This is the opposite of love, the epitome of selfishness. It is a perversion of God's love in our lives.

We are also warned against plotting evil. Too often thoughts devise iniquity. "Your feet run to do evil and rush to murder; your thoughts are only sinning, and wherever you go you leave behind a trail of misery and death" (Isaiah 59:7). This pictures a heart that has become a workshop for the devil. Standing for God puts us right in the middle of a war. Anything that we do not consciously commit to God, Satan will take. We need to bring every thought and every imagination into captivity to Christ (2 Corinthians 10:5). Jesus Christ can control our every thought. If he does not do so, we will plot evil.

Then God warns us about being eager to do wrong. When we devise wickedness in our hearts, we hurry to accomplish it. An evil heart in rebellion against God will be quick and eager to do wrong. This displeases God.

God also despises a false witness. This refers to perjury, the crime of a person who takes the witness stand in a court of law and deliberately lies. This violates God's clear commandment (Exodus 20:16).

So far, most of these things do not cause us much trouble. That warning about plotting evil gets pretty close to us. Occasionally we are a bit haughty. But most of us have not killed anyone. Nor have we been eager to carry out a lot of mischief. Most of us have not been in court. But the seventh thing that God hates catches us all. God hates our "sowing discord among brothers."

The Word of God frequently discusses the alternative to discord, Christian unity. "May God who gives patience, steadiness, and encouragement help you to live in complete harmony with each other—each with the attitude of Christ toward the other. And then all of us can praise the Lord together with one voice, giving glory to God, the Father of our Lord Jesus Christ" (Romans 15:5, 6). "But, dear brothers, I beg you in the name of the Lord Jesus Christ to stop arguing among yourselves. Let there be real harmony so that there won't be splits in the church. I plead with you to be of one mind, united in thought and purpose" (1 Corinthians 1:10). There is to be unity of speech and fellowship among God's children. The expression "united in thought and purpose" describes a bone that has been broken, then put back together so that it fits. God's children are to be perfectly joined together in the same mind, the same judgment.

"Try always to be led along together by the Holy Spirit, and so be at peace with one another" (Ephesians 4:3). "Then make me truly happy by loving each other and agreeing wholeheartedly with each other, working together with one heart and mind and purpose" (Philippians 2:2). "And now this word to all of you: You should be like one big happy family, full of sympathy toward each other, loving one another with tender hearts and humble minds" (1 Peter 3:8). These are but a few of the verses that show God's attitude toward his people's fellowship.

Some Christians are absolute experts at discord. They thrive on tension and sarcasm. They put up roadblocks within the fellowship. They seem to be oblivious to the fact that God says, "I hate discord."

Can you imagine a born-again believer using his

body, his mind, his tongue, and all that he is to create dissension and division rather than health, healing, and unity? Imagine the disappointment when a man created for eternal fellowship with God and partnership with God's children sows discord among the saints. This must be the saddest experience God has to face. God has commissioned his church to spread the gospel to a dying world, but we dissipate our efforts in discord.

If we are to accomplish the task God has set before us, there is no room in our lives for haughtiness, lying, murdering, plotting evil, eagerness to do wrong, being a false witness, or sowing discord among brothers. These are six things the Lord hates—no, seven. We are to avoid them because they are perversions of what God wants for our lives.

The Grace of Humility

The idea of humility was not popular in the ancient world. Humility to people then meant subservience, slavery.

Today we have not progressed beyond that same misconception. Most of us are not complimentary of people who are humble. We equate humility with being timid, reticent, retiring, soft. A humble person is regarded as being easy to persuade or push around.

This is not the biblical view at all. Humility is a grace—it cannot be achieved in our own strength. Humility is given to us by God. It is an outgrowth of our relationship with him.

The writer of Proverbs tells us about humility in the day-to-day affairs of life. "When you remove corrupt men from the king's court, his reign will be just and fair. Don't demand an audience with the king as though you were some powerful prince. It is better to wait for an invitation rather than to be sent back to the end of the line, publicly disgraced! ... Just as it is harmful to eat too much honey, so also it is bad for men to think about all the honors they deserve! A man without self-control is as defenseless as a city with broken-down walls" (25:5-7, 27, 28).

This passage closely parallels Luke 14, where Jesus tells us about a man who went to a wedding feast. The first thing that he did was to sit down beside the guest of honor. His actions said, "I am more important than others. This is where I belong." The host had to go over to him and say, "Friend, would you mind moving to the foot of the table?" Jesus said it's better if we sit at the foot of the table and then are invited to come to the place of honor. Why? "For everyone who tries to honor himself shall be humbled; and he who humbles himself shall be honored" (Luke 14:11).

There is a humility that is desirable, wise, not pretentious. Its opposite is the wrong kind of pride. Not all pride is evil. We should take pride in the way we appear to others and in the way we conduct ourselves. However, we should not have a sense of pride that is overbearing and overwhelming to those around us. That is the opposite of the humility that God gives.

Many of us today have a misapplied pride. It is not wrong for us to want to be noticed or to achieve, or to have a deep desire to belong. What is desperately wrong today is that many of us use shabby means of achieving those desires and so cheapen the desire itself. We distort it, and it becomes an end in and of itself. Everyone wants to get ahead of the next fellow. Everyone wants to achieve more than others. Wallace Hamilton once said that if all the automobile drivers in the United States were lined up bumper to bumper along the highway, 95 percent of them would pull out to pass. We are on a merry-go-round of success. We try to achieve something desirable in undesirable ways. We seem to forget that the only way we can truly achieve success is for God to be himself in us. We must let God make us what we cannot be in ourselves.

EXPRESSIONS OF PRIDE

As we read Proverbs we cannot escape the fact that it has a lot to say about pride, the opposite of true humility. The pointers given there are not for us to use to check up on others, but to check ourselves.

One way pride shows itself is in arrogance. The man in Proverbs 25:5-7 barges into the presence of the king as though he belonged at his right hand, assuming that his importance is significant enough that he can demand a place of great prestige. That's arrogance.

We also find arrogance in pushiness of pride in the mocker. "Mockers are proud, haughty and arrogant" (21:24). A mocker disdains everyone else. To him the whole world is wrong and he is right. Everyone else is out of step but him. He has not humility.

Another expression of pride is contention or strife. "Pride leads to arguments; be humble, take advice and become wise" (13:10). Jesus Christ came to save us from our foolish pride. Yet pride is the most devastating force used by Satan to work against the church. All across America today he causes contention, strife, and confusion in the fellowship of God's people. Whenever people believe they have had a deeper experience than anyone else, or a more biblical one, their pride causes contentions that sweep across a community and tear down the church of God.

Still another fruit of pride is shame and embarrassment. "Proud men end in shame, but the meek become wise" (11:2). Ultimately a proud person is going to be ashamed. He will realize his error and wish to God that he could unravel the web of his life. When he realizes what he has done with the life God left in his care, he will weep.

Summarizing all of these expressions of pride, the Bible tells us that it is sinful. "Pride, lust, and evil actions are all sin" (21:4). The list of seven things that God hates (6:17) includes pride. In fact, we are told, "Pride disgusts the Lord. Take my word for it—proud men shall be punished" (16:5).

Pride's end is destruction. "Pride goes before destruction and haughtiness before a fall" (16:18). "Pride ends in destruction; humility ends in honor" (18:12). The man who is proud and arrogant, who believes himself to be something he is not, will fall. "So be careful. If you are thinking, 'Oh, I would never behave like that'—let this be a warning to you. For you too may fall into sin" (1 Corinthians 10:12).

.

EVIDENCES OF HUMILITY

In his book *Christ in His Church*, William Temple says, "Humility does not mean thinking less of yourself than of other people, nor does it mean having a low opinion of your own gifts. It means freedom from thinking about yourself one way or the other at all."

Humility does not require us to put ourselves down,
or to avoid being concerned about our own interests or
rights. Humility that is greatly occupied with ourselves
and which avows how little we are worth is not Christian humility. It is simply another form of self-pre-
occupation, and a very poor one at that.

Many people go around saying, "I am nobody. I am
so insignificant. I am so unimportant." That is an in-
verted form of pride. It is not Christian humility. Because God loves us, has redeemed us, and lives within
us, we are of great worth. This is an acknowledgment of
fact and is not pride at all.

Humility as revealed in Proverbs manifests itself in a
full and happy life. The humble person is happy, and is
not threatened by other people. "True humility and respect for the Lord lead a man to riches, honor and long
life" (22:4). Fullness of life comes through humility.
Jesus declared, "For anyone who keeps his life for himself shall lose it; and anyone who loses his life for me
shall find it again" (Matthew 16:25). We will lose the
very thing we try to achieve by grasping at it through
pride. But if we will lose ourselves to God and humble
ourselves before him, we will find our lives in Christ.
Fullness of life comes when we give up our rights and
turn them over to God.

A second evidence of humility is a disciplined life.
"Just as it is harmful to eat too much honey, so also it is
bad for men to think about all the honors they deserve!
A man without self-control is as defenseless as a city
with broken-down walls" (25:27, 28). A man who has
no control over his own spirit is not a humble man. If a

man's spirit is undisciplined, he is like a city that is destroyed.

I will never forget walking through the ruins of Waco, Texas, following a devastating tornado. The destruction and tragedy were unimaginable. That is what our lives are like if they are undisciplined. There is no peace, no happiness there. If we have real humility, our lives are under control, and we experience discipline and wholesomeness.

A third evidence of humility is obedience. A humble person is subservient to God. "The wise man is glad to be instructed, but a self-sufficient fool falls flat on his face (10:8). Proverbs 3:1 tells us to remember the instructions we have been given. In so doing we will find favor and good reputation in the sight of God and of man. If, as we come to an awareness of God's purpose and will, we bow our knees obediently to God, that is evidence of humility.

One further evidence of humility is wisdom. "Proud men end in shame, but the meek become wise" (11:2). Wisdom is God's gift to the humble. "A fool thinks he needs no advice, but a wise man listens to others" (12:15). A humble person shows his wisdom by listening to wise counsel. Genuine humility rests on God's Word, not on personal opinion or pet theories.

It is not possible to gain humility by our own efforts. It comes only by faith. We do not get it by flexing our muscles or showing our strength, but by bowing our knees in helplessness before God. Humility cannot be gained by arrogant pride that rests in its own ability and talent, but by simple submission to God's purposes.

Christ demonstrated that kind of humility. "Your attitude should be the kind that was shown us by Jesus Christ, who, though he was God, did not demand and cling to his rights as God, but laid aside his mighty power and glory, taking the disguise of a slave and becoming like men. And he humbled himself even further, going so far as actually to die a criminal's death on a cross" (Philippians 2:5-8). There was a godly kind of pride in his life, yet he was truly humble. He did not demand his rights. He did not come to earth with a fanfare and say, "Hey, everybody, listen to me. I am Jesus Christ superstar."

When he came to earth he took upon himself the form of a servant and was made in the likeness of man. He humbled himself and become obedient, even to the point of death on the cross. "Yet it was because of this that God raised him up to the heights of heaven and gave him a name which is above every other name, that at the name of Jesus every knee shall bow in heaven and on earth and under the earth, and every tongue shall confess that Jesus Christ is Lord, to the glory of God the Father" (Philippians 2:9-11).

By being submissive and suffering misunderstanding, scorn, and death, Jesus Christ triumphed over the false pride of his enemies. That is how he came to be exalted. He humbled himself and God exalted him.

If we want real meaning and purpose in our lives, we need to humble ourselves and permit God to use his power to exalt us according to his will. That is how we gain true humility. The grace of humility comes to us as we trust God.

The Scourge of Laziness

6

Have you ever noticed how much our physical activity (or inactivity) affects our spiritual lives? And that the lazy person is the last one to know he is lazy? If you tell him, he doesn't believe it.

Perhaps that is the reason God speaks so boldly about laziness in the book of Proverbs. It is his desire that we discover our laziness before it is too late. We read, for example, "Take a lesson from the ants, you lazy fellow. Learn from their ways and be wise! For though they have no king to make them work, yet they labor hard all summer, gathering food for the winter. But you—all you do is sleep. When will you wake up? 'Let me sleep a little longer!' Sure, just a little more! And as you sleep, poverty creeps upon you like a robber and destroys you; want attacks you in full armor" (6:6-11).

Laziness is a scourge, a tragedy, a travesty upon human dignity. It is one of the saddest things that can come to the human heart. We will look honestly at it as God's Word pictures it.

EXAMPLE

The lazy person is first of all someone who seldom begins anything himself. "But you—all you do is sleep.
When will you wake up?" (6:9). The lazy person's answer is, "Let me sleep a little longer!" (6:10). He is
always in need of someone to prod him along.

The lazy person does not become lazy with one great,
sudden rebellion. He becomes lazy by inches or min-
utes. Little by little he sinks into laziness. The little
moment, the little time, the little detail that he lets go
by the wayside make him into a sluggard. He becomes
slothful slowly.

"A lazy man won't even dress the game he gets while
hunting, but the diligent man makes good use of everything he finds" (12:27). He goes hunting but never
dresses his game. He does not finish what he starts,
preferring to let someone else do it for him. "Some men
are so lazy they won't even feed themselves!" (19:24).
Because he is a quitter and loves being waited on, "a
lazy man is brother to the saboteur" (18:9). If we hire
such a person, we are the loser. He wastes his time and
energy, and ours. He is a danger to his employer and
his fellow employees.

EXASPERATION

There is little that can be done for the lazy. "The lazy
man won't go out and work. 'There might be a lion
outside!' he says. He sticks to his bed like a door to its
hinges! He is too tired even to lift his food from his dish
to his mouth! Yet in his own opinion he is smarter than

seven wise men" (26:13-16). Can we imagine anything so silly? Even in biblical days, lions didn't come into the city—they remained in the hills. But the lazy man's excuse was that he might be eaten by a lion. Hilarious! Observing the sluggard will wear you out. "He sticks to his bed like a door to its hinges." When we try to get him to do something, he simply vacillates. Like a door on its hinges, he swings back and forth, never going anywhere. We can never make any progress with him. And we cannot tell him anything—he is wise in his own conceit.

It is exasperating to work with a lazy person. Laziness creates some of the most preposterous excuses we can imagine. One lady told me the reason she had not been in church for the last month was that she had had the three-day measles. How do we answer that? One day I knocked on the door of a home and said to the people, "We want you to come to our church. Would you come?"

They replied, "We don't know if we are going to stay in this town or not."

"Well," I asked, "how long have you been here?"

"Nine years."

What could I say? Another lady said to me, "I will tell you why I don't come to church. It is too close for me to get my car out and drive, and it is too far to walk." How do we deal with people like that? It is exasperating. It tears at our hearts. If it were not so tragic, it would be humorous.

The sad thing is that the lazy person believes his own excuses. He has told them so many times, he actually believes them to be true. He has forgotten how ridiculous they sound. Perhaps that is why we are told that the lazy person is beyond counsel. "In his own opinion he is smarter than seven wise men" (26:16). He has convinced himself that he is wiser than anyone else. He doesn't want to be bothered by the facts. His mind is set. In fact, he resents counsel. Thus, the lazy person is beyond help. He seeks no advice. He has all the answers. He knows it all.

The lazy person is also unbelievably selfish. "He sticks to his bed like a door to its hinges! He is too tired even to lift his food from his dish to his mouth!" (26:14, 15). All he is concerned about is getting his rest. He has no one else's interest at heart. He is not concerned for his fellow man, for the kingdom of God, for the rightness of society, or anything else except his own comfort. He wants his meals in bed; he wants somebody to take care of him. He is incredibly selfish. Even worse, the lazy person is the last one to see what kind of person he is. Everyone else knows, but not him. He is too self-centered to see.

EXPERIENCE

What is the experience of the lazy person? "The lazy man longs for many things but his hands refuse to work. He is greedy to get, while the godly love to give!" (21:25, 26). He always wants the possessions or prestige that somebody else has. He craves the place of honor, the place of attainment, the place of favor in the eyes of men. This desire is his downfall.

The lazy person is restless, unhappy, dissatisfied. There is a lack of fulfillment in his life. He is unhappy in his work, in his home, in his social contacts, and even at church. All this because he has never released himself to God.

It is interesting to me how much similarity there is between the drunkard and the sluggard. Proverbs tells us that a person who gives himself to strong drink is irresponsible. So is the lazy person. He cannot be counted on for anything. He is either in poverty or he is like a leech, living off somebody else. That is the experience of the lazy person and the drunkard.

"The way of the slothful man is as a hedge of thorns: but the way of the righteous is made plain" (15:19, KJV). We used to have a pyracantha bush in our yard. I often appreciated the beauty of its berries. One day I was trimming it and discovered that there were also thorns on that bush. It was a painful discovery.

The Bible declares that the lazy man will live a life hedged with thorns. He thinks he will enjoy his bed of leisure and that people will wait upon him. He thinks life will be all that he wants it to be. But the lazy man has a rough road. He will be restless, unhappy. His self-centeredness will keep him from contributing to those about him. He will refuse to face responsibility. His road will be lined with thorns.

EXHORTATION

"Take a lesson from the ants, you lazy fellow. Learn from their ways and be wise! For though they have no

king to make them work, yet they labor hard all summer, gathering food for the winter" (6:6-8). Have you
ever watched a colony of ants at work? If they ever sleep
you would never know it. Able to carry many times
their weight, they move back and forth, clearing their
way, doing their job. They do monumental tasks. The
Holy Spirit tells us to "learn from their ways and be
wise."

This is our challenge. The ant has no overseer, needs
no supervision. The ant needs no prodding; the lazy
man does. He must be constantly pushed and directed.
God exhorts all of us to do the task he has placed before
us. We are to redeem the time and take advantage of
every moment God gives us.

The ant shows us how to work, and how to prepare
for the future. The ant provides meat in summer and
stores food from the harvest for winter. The lazy person
is too self-centered to be aware of time. He often does
one thing when it is time to do something else. He
latches the gate after the calf is already gone.

Do you remember the story of the grasshopper and
the ant? While the ant was working one summer, the
grasshopper was out jumping around and having a
good time. "There is plenty of time," the grasshopper
told himself. When cold weather came, the ant had prepared for winter, but the grasshopper had not. The ant
went down into its warm, cozy anthill. The grasshopper was left outside to freeze and die in the winter cold.

The lazy man, like the grasshopper, flits here and
there, never settling down to do the job that ought to be
done. The lazy man learns, but he learns too late. "I

walked by the field of a certain lazy fellow and saw that it was overgrown with thorns, and covered with weeds; and its walls were broken down. Then, as I looked, I learned this lesson: 'A little extra sleep, a little more slumber, a little folding of the hands to rest' means poverty will break in upon you suddenly like a robber, and violently like a bandit" (24:30-34).

The lazy man is an ordinary man. He is not a freak. He looks the same as anyone else. But by continually making excuses, postponing tasks, and refusing opportunities, his life grinds on to waste and despair. Very casually, the lazy person gradually slips into wastefulness.

The spiritual implications of laziness are staggering to me. Many people seem to be very busy and active physically, yet are spiritually lazy. They spend considerable time in daily Bible study, and love to go to church. But don't ask them to visit a lost neighbor down the street, or to knock on doors in their neighborhood, or to bake a pie for someone whose husband just died. Don't ask them to be part of a ministry to the poor or the underprivileged. The truth is they are spiritually lazy. They have religion, but no spiritual vitality.

"So we must listen very carefully to the truths we have heard, or we may drift away from them" (Hebrews 2:1). When we are spiritually lazy, it does not mean that we rebel against the truth. More likely, we just let it get away from us. We need to be disciplined in our spiritual lives. We need to put our faith into practice by loving people, caring for people, witnessing to people, and sharing the things that God has given us.

"For since the messages from angels have always proved true and people have always been punished for disobeying them, what makes us think that we can escape if we are indifferent to this great salvation announced by the Lord Jesus himself, and passed on to us by those who heard him speak?" (Hebrews 2:2, 3). This passage is not written to the unsaved, but to God's children. It concerns their spiritual vitality and usefulness. If we do not have diligence, discipline, discernment, we will lose, not our eternal salvation, but the joy, beauty, meaning, and satisfaction of that salvation in our hearts. It will be lost because of our spiritual laziness.

A physically lazy person with all his absurd excuses and unbelievable selfishness is a walking tragedy. But it is even more tragic to see a spiritually lazy person. What a travesty it is when a person knows the truth and will not act upon it, when he knows the Word of God and does not live by it or yield his life to it.

The ant redeems the time, reaps the harvest, moves ahead with its assignment. It does this instinctively. It is not lazy. That is how we ought to respond to the Spirit of God in our hearts.

Earth's Greatest Partnership

7

The book of Proverbs links the husband and wife together as a team, a partnership. We read, for example, "Listen to your father and mother. What you learn from them will stand you in good stead; it will gain you many honors" (1:8, 9). The husband and wife work together in the team effort of rearing their children. This pattern continues throughout Proverbs.

In the last chapter, there is the same emphasis on the partnership of marriage. That chapter speaks of the virtuous woman's industry, wisdom, and counsel. It tells about her husband being well-known in the affairs of the city, largely because of her partnership with him in the affairs of life. She cares well for her household. She looks out for the family that the Lord has given her. Her children and her husband praise her. Here we see that a family unit is to walk together before the Lord.

ITS BASIS

What is the basis of marriage? It is precisely at this point that many couples miss the mark of God's ideal for a happy and prosperous marriage. There is increasing evidence of the disruption of the home in our society today, as shown by the increasing divorce and desertion rate, as well as the growing number of couples who decide to live together without tying themselves down to the legal aspects of marriage.

The true basis for partnership in marriage is faith in God. In the Bible there are constant admonitions to young men not to link their lives with ungodly women. For a home to be built on a proper foundation, there must not be an unequal yoke. The basis for marriage is shared commitment to God. "The man who finds a wife finds a good thing; she is a blessing to him from the Lord" (18:22). God is a part of marriage and family life. "A father can give his sons homes and riches, but only the Lord can give them understanding wives" (19:14).

If a man trusts in God, if he is loyal to God, his children reap the benefits. "Reverence for God gives a man deep strength; his children have a place of refuge and security" (14:26). "It is a wonderful heritage to have an honest father" (20:7). Trust in God brings refuge, strength, security, honesty. There is no basis for the right kind of marriage until God is enthroned in the lives of both husband and wife.

Last year, there were more divorce petitions filed than marriage licenses in Dallas, Texas. That is characteristic of the society in which we live. If our marriages are not properly based, they cannot bring glory and honor to the Lord. As a result, the happiness of heart that we desire from marriage will be elusive, always just beyond our reach.

It is a mistake even to consider marrying someone who is not saved. It would be better not to marry. It would save a great deal of heartache. Marriage to an unbeliever violates the principles of the Word of God. When God tells us not to marry someone who is not saved, he does it to protect us. He does not want to hurt us, nor does he want us to hurt ourselves. He does not want to keep us from marrying the one we ought to have. He wants us to marry the one who will make us happiest. Anything less would be tragedy.

ITS EXPRESSION

This partnership expresses itself in friendship. "Only wisdom from the Lord can save a man from the flattery of prostitutes; these girls have abandoned their husbands and flouted the laws of God" (2:16, 17). The word rendered "husband" in this passage is translated "friend" elsewhere (16:28; 17:9). A woman who has gone astray has forsaken the friendship of her husband. Husbands and wives should, obviously, be friends. The alternative? Contention, strife, unhappiness. Many couples love each other, yet have trouble putting up with each other.

Love, physical and otherwise, is important to the marriage partnership. The writer of Proverbs instructs a husband, 'Let her charms and tender embrace satisfy you. Let her love alone fill you with delight" (5:19). There is a very intimate physical relationship between the husband and wife. The sexual appetite of the human body is of God, and so is to be protected as a holy gift that is to be reserved for marriage. God gave us this physical marriage relationship so we can be "ravished" (5:19, KJV) by the love of our mate. It is a beautiful expression of oneness, unity.

Its abuse is an affront to God himself. When it is taken out of its proper perspective and perverted, it becomes sinful, ugly. Sin is an abuse of something that is right, the misuse of something that is holy. Any sin can be traced back to a holy admonition of God that has been abused and perverted. We misdirect God's admonitions for our own selfish satisfaction—and that's sin.

What a thrill it is to enter into marriage in purity and to discover the joys of the physical relationship of love for the first time under the leadership of the Holy Spirit. This warms the heart, and tightens the bonds of love and friendship that will strengthen any home. Keep yourself for that time. Such an expression of earth's greatest partnership brings harmony, an ideal emphasized throughout Proverbs. A relaxed atmosphere in the home requires proper expressions of love.

This partnership also expresses itself in faithfulness. "Drink from your own well, my son—be faithful and true to your wife. Why should you beget children with women of the street? Why share your children with those outside your home? Let your manhood be a blessing; rejoice in the wife of your youth. Let her charms and tender embrace satisfy you. Let her love alone fill you with delight. Why delight yourself with prostitutes, embracing what isn't yours? For God is closely watching you and he weighs carefully everything you do" (5:15-21). To begin and continue marriage in the way God intends we must be faithful to God and to the mate he has given us.

As God gives children to a marriage, there is further opportunity to express our commitment to him. We can express our love to God through our care and concern for our children. "For I, too, was once a son, tenderly loved by my mother as an only child, and the companion of my father. He told me never to forget his words. 'If you follow them,' he said, 'you will have a long and happy life' " (4:3, 4). When God gives us children, he makes husband and wife partners in instructing them. "My son, listen to me and do as I say, and you will have a long, good life. I would have you learn this great fact: that a life of doing right is the wisest life there is. If you live that kind of life, you'll not limp or stumble as you run. Carry out my instructions; don't forget them, for they will lead you to real living" (4:10-13). Children need counsel, guidance, instruction. They need to be brought up in the nurture and admonition of the Lord. We are to carefully instruct them.

We are also to discipline our children. "Young man, do not resent it when God chastens and corrects you, for his punishment is proof of his love. Just as a father punishes a son he delights in to make him better, so the Lord corrects you" (3:11, 12). If we love our children, we will correct them, thus keeping them from evil ways. "If you refuse to discipline your son, it proves you don't love him; for if you love him you will be prompt to punish him" (13:24). "Scolding and spanking a child helps him to learn. Left to himself, he brings shame to his mother.... Discipline your son and he will give you happiness and peace of mind" (29:15, 17).

ITS VIOLATION

In the same passage that admonished us to be faithful in this partnership we read, "Listen, son of mine, to what I say. Listen carefully. Keep these thoughts ever in mind; let them penetrate deep within your heart, for they will mean real life for you, and radiant health. Above all else, guard your affections. For they influence everything else in your life" (4:20-23).

Throughout Proverbs we are urged not to violate the relationship between husband and wife. We may sometimes ask ourselves, "Why not?" In our own minds we can't find sufficient reason for faithfulness. Even our friends aren't much help. Worse, we often refuse to ask God for assistance—perhaps because we don't want it.

God declares that if we violate our marriage partnership, we will receive dishonor and shame. "But the man who commits adultery is an utter fool, for he destroys his own soul. Wounds and constant disgrace are his lot, for the woman's husband will be furious in his jealousy, and he will have no mercy on you in his day of vengeance. You won't be able to buy him off no matter what you offer" (6:32-35). The law of God is sure— infidelity brings dishonor. "For a prostitute will bring a man to poverty, and an adulteress may cost him his very life" (6:26). Disregard for the sanctity of marriage may rob a man of his life. Statistics about venereal disease, the so-called "eternal triangles," and the like proves this possibility. Violation of the marriage relationship is indeed a serious, even disastrous matter. "Only wisdom from the Lord can save a man from the flattery of prostitutes; these girls have abandoned their husbands and flouted the laws of God. Their houses lie along the road to death and hell. The men who enter them are doomed. None of these men will ever be the same again" (2:16-19).

"Can a man hold fire against his chest and not be burned? Can he walk on hot coals and not blister his feet?" (6:27, 28). Obviously not! Anyone who steps barefooted on hot coals will be burned—without exception. And anyone who violates earth's greatest partnership will suffer for it. "O my son, trust my advice—stay away from prostitutes. For a prostitute is a deep and narrow grave. Like a robber, she waits for her victims as one after another become unfaithful to their wives" (23:26-28). A person caught in a deep ditch or a narrow grave cannot get out without help. God, in his gracious mercy, offers to come to our aid when we turn to him. His strength can keep us from falling into the pitfalls that would ruin our marriage.

If people who claim to know Jesus Christ would be true to their marriage commitment, they could revolutionize America. They could reverse the trend of divorce in our society. God's power can be seen in strong marriages. The problem with America is not only that our society is godless; the church is in many ways godless too. Too many people who have their names on church rolls and are active in the fellowship

of the church are neglecting their marriage respon-
sibilities. Marital disaster in our land is the result, and
God's people are contributing to it. There were over
one million divorces filed in the United States in 1975.

If America goes down the drain, we Christians must
share the blame. We have not been true to God. The
experience that Abraham and Lot had concerning
Sodom and Gomorrah tells us that God will spare a
great city even if there are only a handful of righteous
people in it. But when people who claim to know God
become unrighteous and violate his commandments,
there is no escape. Their society is destined for disaster.
If we Christians would commit ourselves to God, we
could save America.

ITS RESULT

The result of earth's greatest partnership lived in commitment to God is happiness in the home. Such a home
exhibits wisdom, strength, prosperity. "Any enterprise
is built by wise planning, becomes strong through
common sense, and profits wonderfully by keeping
abreast of the facts" (24:3, 4). The home that is loyal to
God will have wisdom in its day-to-day affairs. It will
be winsome and wholesome in the ways of the Lord.

That home's love and reverence for God sets it on a
higher plane than other homes. "Better a little with reverence for God, than great treasure and trouble with it.
It is better to eat soup with someone you love than steak
with someone you hate" (15:16, 17). A home that is
based on the Word of God and commitment to God will

express itself in the beauty of friendship, happy contentment.

When we come to the end of our lifetimes and look back to the happiest times, we will discover that they were the struggling years, the times when we couldn't afford luxuries. We didn't have much money, but we were happy. We may have had to eat beans and cornbread, but we had love and contentment for dessert. We had a reverence for God and for each other. God was doing something with us and in us. That is the kind of home that God desires for us.

Many of us have many things, yet are not happy. In fact, we're miserable and aren't sure why. We have been led to believe that if we had a new house, we would be happy—or a swimming pool, or a new car, or a better position at work, or.... Yet life continues to be a rat race, a race we seem to be losing. When we reach one plateau, we just hunger for something else. It will be that way all of our lives until and unless we are genuinely committed to Christ. Things will not improve until he brings the pieces together for us. Only in him can we be truly happy.

When we are happy, our homes will be happy too. "A dry crust eaten in peace is better than steak every day along with argument and strife" (17:1). Quietness of heart results in peace, contentment, and satisfaction. God can build this into our hearts. Only he can bring us the happiness we seek.

Perhaps you're saying, "I have a problem. I'm divorced. I've already blown it." God can put the pieces back together again. He can bring the forgiveness that you need. He can give you a fresh start in life.

Someone else may say, "My mate is not saved. What should I do?" "If a Christian has a wife who is not a Christian, but she wants to stay with him anyway, he must not leave her or divorce her. And if a Christian woman has a husband who isn't a Christian, and he wants her to stay with him, she must not leave him. For perhaps the husband who isn't a Christian may become a Christian with the help of his Christian wife. And the wife who isn't a Christian may become a Christian with the help of her Christian husband. Otherwise, if the family separates, the children might never come to know the Lord; whereas a united family may, in God's plan, result in the children's salvation" (1 Corinthians 7:12-14). If we lift up our homes to him and live godly lives in the home, salvation will come to that unsaved husband or wife.

There is no situation that is beyond hope, no situation too far gone for God to correct. If we will bring ourselves to God, if we will come to the foot of the cross and there bow our knees and open our hearts to him, God will mend our lives. He can bring happiness, contentment, peace to our homes. He wants us to experience earth's greatest partnership in its fullness.

Heaven's
Greatest
Trust

8

The book of Proverbs is counsel given from a father to his son. It can apply equally to a mother and her daughter. But all of us have a stake in what is said. For the young, Proverbs is an admonition. It is a reminder to commit our lives to God as we mature through the youthful years of our lives. For those of us who have passed into adulthood, Proverbs is given to help us counsel those who are young. That is our charge.

Children are not our own. We should see them as a sacred trust from God, a gift from heaven. God has entrusted them to us for the shaping of their hearts and minds, the molding of their character.

"The father of a godly man has cause for joy—what pleasure a wise son is! So give your parents joy!" (23:24, 25). Children are God's gift of happiness to our lives. "Children are a gift from God; they are his reward" (Psalm 127:3). Our children will either bring joy or sorrow into our hearts. "Happy is the man with a levelheaded son; sad the mother of a rebel" (10:1). "It's no fun to be a rebel's father.... A rebellious son is a grief to his father and a bitter blow to his mother" (17:21, 25).

If we view children as a trust from God, we will put our full effort into their training and guiding. They will be a delight to us, a joy. But if we shirk that responsibility, our children will be a burden to us. We must either exercise the influence and discipline that God intended for us as parents, or our children will bring us sorrow. Surely we want them to be a joy. How can that happen? Read on.

EXAMPLE

Parents are to be examples to their children. Too many of us say, "Do as I say, not as I do." We expect our children to have good manners without ever having seen them practiced. We expect them to be kind without ever having experienced kindness. The example of the parents affects them more than we know.

Remember—if a home is to be what it ought to be, it must be based upon God and upon the godly principles he has revealed. "Unless the Lord builds a house, the builders' work is useless. Unless the Lord protects a city, sentries do no good" (Psalm 127:1). This holds true in the matter of raising children. We need to provide them with an example in godliness. "It is a wonderful heritage to have an honest father" (20:7). The greatest obligation we have toward our children is that we be Christians, committed children of God who are maturing and growing in his grace. Our example in godliness will be rewarded with the blessings of God upon our families.

We cannot expect our children to have spiritual qualities we as parents don't demonstrate in our own lives. If we send our children to church instead of taking them, if we expect others to pray with them instead of kneeling with them at home and church, if we expect the church to teach them the Word of God instead of teaching it to them in our homes, we are failing in our task. As a result, we will miss out on blessing our families and the world through the children God has given to us.

We are responsible to live godly lives before them. It is our responsibility, not somebody else's. We cannot pass it on to someone else, or to the church. It is a trust God has given to us.

We are not only to be godly examples to our children, but loving ones. "For I, too, was once a son, tenderly loved by my mother as an only child, and the companion of my father" (4:3). I wonder if our children know we love them. Sometimes all our children hear are the orders and the threats. One of the saddest things I experience occurs when a young person comes to me and says, "I never heard my mother and father tell me they loved me. They never gave me a hug of affection or a kiss of love." As parents we need to demonstrate our love, for each other and for our children. It will help them to see that their parents are kind and compassionate toward each other. We must provide such a context of concern in which our children can grow.

We are also to be examples of giving. I'm not talking

about money, but sharing ourselves with our children. "Scolding and spanking a child helps him to learn. Left to himself, he brings shame to his mother" (29:15). Too often we leave our children alone. We use television as a babysitter, an easy way to get our children out of our hair. Our children need attention at all hours and in all ways. No matter how inconvenient, we must minister to them. We may be tired when one of our children needs us, but we must be available. Unknowingly and unwittingly many of us give a picture of selfishness to our children. We need to rather give them an example of giving ourselves to others.

This includes teaching our children, counseling them. "Young man, obey your father and your mother. Tie their instructions around your finger so you won't forget. Take to heart all of their advice. Every day and all night long their counsel will lead you and save you from harm; when you wake up in the morning, let their instructions guide you into the new day. For their advice is a beam of light directed into the dark corners of your mind to warn you of danger and to give you a good life" (6:20-23). We are to teach and show the truth to our children.

This requires us to discipline them. We do not necessarily teach truth by using a belt or some other physical punishment. Our instruction may use some other kind of discipline. But whatever its form, we must discipline our children. If we don't, they will become rebels, and society will discipline them in one way or another. Our nation is in turmoil and revolution today because respect for authority has not been taught in the home.

Too many Christians' homes have failed to set a sufficient example for their children.

EXHORTATION

We are responsible to exhort, warn, guide our children. For example, we are to exhort them to be industrious. "A wise youth makes hay while the sun shines, but what a shame to see a lad who sleeps away his hour of opportunity" (10:5). We are not to give our children everything they want. We must help them learn not to be lazy, to exhort them not to be idle. If they don't learn that in the home, they may never learn it at all.

We are to encourage purity. "Only wisdom from the Lord can save a man from the flattery of prostitutes; these girls have abandoned their husbands and flouted the laws of God. Their houses lie along the road to death and hell. The men who enter them are doomed. None of these men will ever be the same again. Follow the steps of the godly instead, and stay on the right path, for only good men enjoy life to the full; evil men lose the good things they might have had, and they themselves shall be destroyed" (2:16-22). We must warn our children about inevitable temptations, and also keep ourselves pure as an example to them.

God's emphasis on purity is not meant to keep us from having fun, or to curb legitimate desires. God wants us to get the most out of life. Everything in the world, if it is used rightly, is good. But sin twists good, making it evil and harmful. That's why we have the admonition to guard our love and our minds. We too can pervert good and make it evil—that's immorality.

The physical relationship of husband and wife is beautiful, holy, ordained of God as an expression of love. Its fulfillment and completion, however, is reserved for marriage. That is God's design. Any perversion or abuse of it is sin. The person who flouts it will do so to his own harm, shame, and despair. Day after day there are individuals and couples who tell me of the guilt plaguing them because of premarital sex. Perhaps they rationalized that they were going to get married, so it's all right. Or, "We will be married anyway in God's eyes." Using this rationalization of the devil, they engaged in impurity and sabotaged their own lives. We need to tell our children why they should preserve their purity for marriage.

We also need to teach our children that truth is not just something we believe, it is something we do. We should express and show our love to our families. If we say we love them but never buy groceries or give them any attention, we reveal that we don't mean what we say. Concerning instructions received from parents, we read, "Write them down, and also keep them deep within your heart" (7:3). These instructions ought to be in our (and our children's) hearts and thoughts, and should exhibit themselves in our actions.

We are also to teach our children to be respectful. We have gotten far away from that in our society, but "listen to your father's advice and don't despise an old mother's experience" (23:22).

If we do not show proper respect for others, great

tragedy and heartache will come to us. "There are those who curse their father and mother, and feel themselves faultless despite their many sins. They are proud beyond description, arrogant, disdainful. They devour the poor with teeth as sharp as knives! There are two things never satisfied, like a leech forever craving more: no, three things! no, four! Hell, the barren womb, a barren desert, fire. A man who mocks his father and despises his mother shall have his eye plucked out by ravens and eaten by vultures" (30:11-17). "God puts out the light of the man who curses his father or mother" (20:20).

If we do not respect others, we cannot respect ourselves. If we cannot respect ourselves, we cannot live happily. This is one of the most important things that we can teach our children.

EXPECTATION

What do we expect for our children? What can we dream for them?

Children taught God's ways can expect a long life. "My son, never forget the things I've taught you. If you want a long and satisfying life, closely follow my instructions" (3:1). "My son, listen to me and do as I say, and you will have a long, good life" (4:10). We want our children to enjoy life. We want them to have as many years as possible. We can help them achieve those prospects by committing our lives to God. We can train our children in the ways of the Lord, and so develop in them the characteristics that bring longevity.

Our children will also live in contentment if they are raised in the nurture and admonition of the Lord. Regardless of what possessions they may or may not have, they will have peace, because the favor of God will rest upon them. "If you want favor with both God and man, and a reputation for good judgment and common sense, then trust the Lord completely; don't ever trust yourself" (3:4, 5). "Have two goals: wisdom—that is, knowing and doing right—and common sense. Don't let them slip away, for they fill you with living energy, and are a feather in your cap. They keep you safe from defeat and disaster and from stumbling off the trail. With them on guard you can sleep without fear; you need not be afraid of disaster or the plots of wicked men, for the Lord is with you; he protects you" (3:21-26).

That's what I want for my children. I want them to be able to sleep at night and not be afraid. I want them to know that wherever they go, God is there, walking with them every step of the way. We can expect this kind of life for our children if we are the kind of parents God wants us to be.

Children are God's gift to us. We owe them our best, but cannot be at our best unless God is in control of our lives. We must commit our hearts to God if we are to be worthy of carrying heaven's greatest trust.

The Way of Life

9

The Bible is a book of contrasts—between God and Satan, good and evil, light and darkness, life and death. Proverbs especially zeroes in on life and death.

In the book of Proverbs "death" does not simply mean the end of physical life. If a person turns his back on God, he endures a form of death even while he lives. Death is a shadow that darkens the life of an individual who rebels against God. It brings envy, anguish, despair, disillusionment, depression.

In contrast, life is given to us by God. Jesus said, "The thief's purpose is to steal, kill and destroy. My purpose is to give life in all its fullness" (John 10:10). That is the message of the Word of God, of Proverbs. God wants us to come alive, to enjoy life in all its abundance. "For their advice is a beam of light directed into the dark corners of your mind to warn you of danger and to give you a good life" (6:23). "The road of the godly leads upward, leaving hell behind" (15:24). God wants us to walk in the heavenlies, to breathe the air of eternity, to have his life.

The tragedy of tragedies occurs when we don't experience life as God intended it. Consider how many Christians are depressed, defeated, discouraged. For many, life is dull and dreary. Yet God wants us to have abundant life.

FULFILLMENT

God wants us to have a full life. The book of Proverbs reveals several aspects of this fulfillment.

God wants to give us a long life on this earth. He does this through the wisdom he gives to us. "Wisdom gives: A long, good life, riches, honor, pleasure, peace" (3:16). "My son, listen to me and do as I say, and you will have a long, good life" (4:10). "I, Wisdom, will make the hours of your day more profitable and the years of your life more fruitful" (9:11).

If we live as God desires, we will enjoy long life. That does not mean that every individual is going to live a long time. We all have known godly people who died in their youth or early adulthood. But generally godliness builds virtues into us that add years to our lives. God wants us to live all our lives to the fullest.

God wants us to be happy, satisfied, joyful in life. He wants us to have wisdom and common sense, "for they fill you with living energy, and are a feather in your cap" (3:22). Here is a life that cannot be defeated, a life that meets obstacles and says, "Praise God, he will get us over them." We can view our difficulties as opportunities to let God do something exciting in our lives.

This happiness can be seen. "So shall they be life unto thy soul, and grace to thy neck" (3:22, KJV).

"Grace to thy neck" means "beauty to your appearance." When we're happy, our faces reflect it. There should be something distinctively different about us that people can see. We often go about frowning, but we should be walking displays of the joy of the Lord.

God also wants us to have peace of mind. It is from our hearts that the real issues of life arise. "A relaxed attitude lengthens a man's life; jealousy rots it away" (14:30). God gives us a tranquil heart when we enter into his life. It is a relief to know that what happens to us is God's problem, not ours. If tragedy comes, God will bring good out of it. He has promised this. God has obligated himself to bring good out of all our experiences, to direct our lives. He wants to give us a life that is at peace and at ease.

God also wants to give us his *wisdom*, the ability to apply knowledge so we enjoy life at its best. "For whoever finds me [Wisdom] finds life and wins approval from the Lord" (8:35).

FORGIVENESS

Psychologists tell us that one of the greatest problems facing people today is the problem of guilt. Guilt is a terrifying pursuer that never gives up. The only solution is divine forgiveness, and that's what God offers to us.

"Iniquity is atoned for by mercy and truth; evil is avoided by reverence for God" (16:6). No matter what our past holds, when we come to Jesus Christ he forgives us. "He has removed our sins as far away from us as the east is from the west" (Psalm 103:12).

Someone might say, "You don't understand. I killed a man." God forgives murderers. Another may say, "I'm guilty of immorality that has destroyed my family." Or "I've been dishonest and I've said things that hurt people deeply. The gap is so wide, it can never be bridged." It does not matter. If we will bring it to God, he will forgive and remove our guilt. Bring your sins to God—he will abundantly pardon. He doesn't forgive us because we deserve it. He does it out of his mercy, because he is love. All we have to do is repent.

FELLOWSHIP

Once we have received forgiveness, we enter into fellowship with God and his people. "For whoever finds me finds life and wins approval from the Lord" (8:35). We were created by God and for God. Apart from him nothing can satisfy the longing in the human heart. If we have money, or knowledge, or status, we want more. Until our hearts find God, they will never be content.

We can experience spiritual satisfaction and fulfillment daily. "Reverence for God gives life, happiness, and protection from harm" (19:23).

Throughout Proverbs, there is a play on the word "life." "Wisdom is a tree of life to those who eat her fruit; happy is the man who keeps on eating it" (3:18). "Hope deferred makes the heart sick; but when dreams come true at last, there is life and joy.... The advice of a wise man refreshes like water from a mountain spring.

Those accepting it become aware of the pitfalls on ahead" (13:12-14). "Reverence for the Lord is a fountain of life; its waters keep a man from death" (14:27). "Wisdom is a fountain of life to those possessing it, but a fool's burden is his folly" (16:22). Wisdom is called a tree of life, a fountain of life, a mountain spring of life. What does this mean?

In Genesis 2 and 3 we read about the tree of life. Elsewhere we read of the water of life (John 4:10; 7:38) and the fountain of life. The tree of life was the key to immortality. The water of life or the fountain of life was a river that flowed by the throne of God, giving it grace and beauty. The psalmist wrote about God saying, "For you are the Fountain of life; our light is from your Light" (Psalm 36:9). And, "There is a river of joy flowing through the City of our God—the sacred home of the God above all gods. God himself is living in that City; therefore it stands unmoved despite the *turmoil* everywhere" (Psalm 46:4, 5). The tree of life and the water of life are keys to immortality and fellowship with God. The river of life sustains God's children.

In paradise man lost his closeness to God, his fellowship with God. God wanted to share intimate harmony with man, but man sinned. He lost the tree of life and the river of life, and is still separated from them. When Jesus returns again, the tree of life and the water of life will be reestablished in God's kingdom. In the meantime, we can recapture a little of it right now.

We do not have to wait until eternity to walk with God. We can have life and fellowship with him now, through faith in the finished work of Jesus Christ. We can have a foretaste of heaven. It will not be like the experience of Adam in Eden or like that of the millennial saints. But we can know the life and fellowship of God right now.

That is what the Apostle Paul meant when he said that when we believe we are "sealed with that Holy Spirit of promise, which is the earnest of our inheritance" (Ephesians 1:13, 14, KJV). The word "earnest" means "down payment." It is part of the purchase price, paid toward the fulfilled purchase. We can have a taste of eternity here and now. We can walk with the Lord now.

God wants us to live out of the abundance of his grace instead of the poverty of our own merits. He wants us to walk in the glory of eternal life here and now, to walk in the heavenlies. Indeed we are already seated in heavenly places with Jesus Christ. That is the life that God has given us—a life of forgiveness and fulfillment.

The Menace of Death

10

We die long before we're buried. So says Proverbs. Proverbs mentions death almost forty times. It doesn't view death merely as a single event at the end of life when we physically stop breathing and are buried in the ground. It includes that, but death is a shadow that hangs over all of life. If we do not live life to its fullest, in one form or another we experience death.

"The wicked man is doomed by his own sin; they are ropes that catch and hold him. He shall die because he will not listen to the truth; he has let himself be led away into incredible folly" (5:22, 23). This passage sets the stage for the biblical view of death as presented in Proverbs. The wicked and sinful man is held captive by his sins.

DEATH OF THE BODY

"Evil men lose the good things they might have had, and they themselves shall be destroyed" (2:22). Evil men die. This is the death of the body. To put it another way, "When an evil man dies, his hopes all perish, for they are based upon this earthly life" (11:7). When a wicked man dies physically, he has nothing ahead of him except hell (spiritual death). "The godly have a refuge when they die, but the wicked are crushed by their sins" (14:32).

Each one of us has a date with physical death, a date 5,000 people keep every hour. The moment we come into the world, we begin the process of dying. All men, whether godly or wicked, die.

If physical death was all we had to fear, death would not be much of a menace. But the death of the body is only a small part of the story.

DEATH OF THE SPIRIT

"The good man finds life; the evil man, death" (11:19). We are all drawn toward death, because we are sinners. "When Adam sinned, sin entered the entire human race. His sin spread death throughout all the world, so everything began to grow old and die, for all sinned" (Romans 5:12). That is the death of the spirit.

The Apostle Paul described spiritual death. "And you hath he quickened, who were dead in trespasses and sins" (Ephesians 2:1, KJV). "Their closed hearts are full of darkness; they are far away from the life of God because they have shut their minds against him, and they cannot understand his ways. They don't care anymore about right and wrong and have given themselves over to impure ways. They stop at nothing, being driven by their evil minds and reckless lusts" (Ephesians 4:18, 19). They are cut off from the life of God. They are physically alive, but spiritually dead. "When these men join you at the love feasts of the church, they are evil smears among you, laughing and carrying on, gorging and stuffing themselves without a thought for others. They are like clouds blowing over dry land without giving rain, promising much, but producing nothing. They are like fruit trees without any fruit at picking time. They are not only dead, but doubly dead, for they have been pulled out, roots and all, to be burned. All they leave behind them is shame and disgrace like the dirty foam left along the beach by wild waves. They wander around looking as bright as stars, but ahead of them is the everlasting gloom and darkness that God has prepared for them" (Jude 12, 13).

Spiritual death is the result of rebellion against God. Two men walking down a road may be the same size and the same age. From all outward appearances they may appear to be equally alive. Yet the Word of God says that one is alive if he knows God and the other is dead if he is still in his sin.

One reason our world is in turmoil is because those in places of leadership are spiritually dead. A spiritual darkness clouds their lives. There is nothing more tragic in all of life than to be separated from the grace of God. That is why Jesus Christ left all the glories of heaven and came to earth. He came to bring forgiveness of sins, to reconcile us to God and give us eternal life.

If we haven't experienced new birth in Christ, we don't have eternal life. Without Christ we will spend eternity cut off from the grace, presence, and fellowship of God.

A man dies spiritually when he sins, when he turns against God. He develops a particular attitude toward life, an attitude which depresses his spirits. Concerning wicked women, Proverbs says, "Their houses lie along the road to death and hell" (2:18). "The wicked man ... shall die because he will not listen to the truth; he has let himself be led away into incredible folly" (5:22, 23). Spiritual death keeps man from meaning and purpose in life. "For whoever finds me [Wisdom] finds life and wins approval from the Lord. But the one who misses me has injured himself irreparably. Those who refuse me show they love death" (8:35, 36).

Spiritual death results in depression, discouragement, despair. It causes unhappiness. It brings pressures that drive us out of our minds. It keeps us up nights. It makes us lose our desire to go on living.

The menace of death may cast a shadow upon us so severely and deeply that we cannot see the sunlight of God's love. We may have physical life, but we cannot enjoy it. We may want to better ourselves, but we do not have the power or the strength to do it.

Proverbs tell us that followers of wicked women "don't realize that her former guests are now citizens of hell" (9:18). A person can experience death without dying. He can experience hell without being there. When we are saved, we have foretastes of heaven. We enjoy love and fellowship that are previews of what God is going to give us over there. When we gather together to sing, rejoice, and worship, we feel the touch of God upon our lives. That is a down payment of what we are going to have later.

The opposite is also true. When unbelievers experience separation from God, and the touch of Satan is in their lives, they experience foretastes of hell, a down payment of eternal separation from God. They receive something of the judgment of God right now. A person who rejects the grace of God will experience some of the pains of eternal death now. The Apostle Paul declared that the woman who lives in pleasure is dead while she lives (1 Timothy 5:6). She is dead even though she has physical life. "So whoever has God's Son has life; whoever does not have his Son, does not have life" (1 John 5:12). There is an aroma of death in his life. "Following after the Holy Spirit leads to life and peace, but following after the old nature leads to death" (Romans 8:6).

The realm of death invades each of our experiences. Every time we spend a minute in envy, we spend an hour in anguish. Our sins pay us in living death. That's why we need to stay close to God, fellowshiping with him. We are to walk in the light as he is in the light; "then we have wonderful fellowship and joy with each other, and the blood of Jesus his Son cleanses us from every sin" (1 John 1:7). The moment we get away from fellowship with God, we begin to experience some form of death.

We bring most of our maladies, depressions, and discouragements on ourselves because we have separated ourselves from the life and fellowship of God. As we do, we experience death.

"Before every man there lies a wide and pleasant road that seems right but ends in death" (14:12). This does not refer to physical death, but to the death of the soul and spirit. The man who thinks he is doing right in his own eyes is a man who soon discovers that the end of his own dreams and ambitions is death and defeat, because he does not know God. Whenever we lean upon our own understanding, we will be frustrated. That is the menace of death.

Dr. George W. Truett, in his book *The Quest for Souls,* tells of a prominent citizen of Dallas who came to the Truett home at 2:00 one morning. He told Dr. Truett that his drinking problem was tearing his family apart. His wife demanded that he kick the habit or she would leave him. He had to stop drinking, yet he couldn't stop. That's a story of death.

It is a familiar story to all of us. "When I want to do good, I don't; and when I try not to do wrong, I do it anyway. Now if I am doing what I don't want to, it is plain where the trouble is: sin still has me in its evil grasp" (Romans 7:19, 20). One of the ways to punish a murderer in the Roman Empire was to chain the corpse to him. Everywhere that murderer went he had to drag the corpse. In time that corpse would begin to decay and putrefy, and the disease of that dead body would spread to the body of the murderer. He was chained to death. We cannot imagine anything worse than that.

The Apostle Paul said, "That is like me. That is the way I am. I am chained to a body of death. There is a menace of death that hangs over me. When I want to do good and when I do not want to do evil, I do it anyway. Who can deliver me from this death?" Then he climaxes that seventh chapter of Romans by saying, "Thank God! It has been done by Jesus Christ our Lord. He has set me free" (7:25). Jesus Christ is the answer to death.

If we are living in fear of death, the oppression of sin, it is by our own choice. God has given us a way of escape. We do not have to be defeated or discouraged. We can escape death by turning to Jesus Christ. He said the hour is coming and now is when the dead will hear the voice of God, and "those who listen shall live" (John 5:25). He wants us to come alive. Any other "life" is just some form of death.

Jesus Christ wants us to escape the menace of death and enter into the eternal life he gives to those who come to him.

God's Financial Counsel

God wants us to know how to deal with the sticky problems of life. He even gives us counsel about our financial affairs, our earthly treasures. He not only wants us to be saved, he wants us to live happily and prosperously after we are saved. Because our personal money problems are often at the root of many other problems we face, we need God's help.

"I [Wisdom] love all who love me. Those who search for me shall surely find me. Unending riches, honor, justice and righteousness are mine to distribute. My gifts are better than the purest gold or sterling silver! My paths are those of justice and right. Those who love and follow me are indeed wealthy. I fill their treasuries" (8:17-21). God is interested in our wealth. But he is even more concerned that we understand that earthly riches are mere symbols of eternal riches, his goal for us.

Jesus said, "Don't store up treasures here on earth where they can erode away or may be stolen. Store them in heaven where they will never lose their value, and are safe from thieves. If your profits are in heaven your heart will be there too" (Matthew 6:19, 20). "Then Peter said to him, 'We left everything to follow you. What will we get out of it?' And Jesus replied, 'When I, the Messiah, shall sit upon my glorious throne in the Kingdom, you my disciples shall certainly sit on twelve thrones judging the twelve tribes of Israel. And anyone who gives up his home, brothers, sisters, father, mother, wife, children, or property, to follow me, shall receive a hundred times as much in return, and shall have eternal life. But many who are first now will be last then; and some who are last now will be first then' " (Matthew 19:27-30). We will receive dividends in eternity. God wants us to have wealth that is lasting, durable, eternal.

EARTHLY WEALTH AND HAPPINESS

Earthly wealth or money can never by itself bring happiness. For one thing, there is no satisfaction in it. "Trust in your money and down you go! Trust in God and flourish as a tree!" (11:28). Earthly wealth does not bring growth, fulfillment, purpose, satisfaction to life. John D. Rockefeller reportedly was asked, "How much money does it take to satisfy a man?" He replied, "Just a little more." God warns us that if our obsession in life is for material wealth, we will never be happy.

Earthly wealth cannot buy salvation. "Your riches won't help you on Judgment Day; only righteousness counts then" (11:4). A man can never be happy until he is saved and is brought into fellowship with God. When judgment comes, rich and poor alike will stand before God. If we do not know God, we will be lost, no matter how large our bank account.

Earthly wealth is not even permanent. "Don't weary yourself trying to get rich. Why waste your time? For riches can disappear as though they had the wings of a bird!" (23:4, 5). A dewdrop is just as beautiful as a diamond. The difference in the value is the permanence. But even diamonds don't last forever. Whoever builds his life around material riches will find that happiness always eludes him.

A man cannot be happy when he is a slave, and earthly wealth enslaves man. If he has too much, he says, "I don't need God." If he doesn't have enough, he curses God. He is out of control either way. Perhaps it is best to pray, "First, help me never to tell a lie. Second, give me neither poverty nor riches! Give me just enough to satisfy my needs! For if I grow rich, I may become content without God. And if I am too poor, I may steal, and thus insult God's holy name" (30:8, 9). Agur, author of Proverbs 30, prayed that God would give him enough to be full, but not enough to be greedy or desperate.

"Just as the rich rule the poor, so the borrower is servant to the lender" (22:7). Some of us may have too much, some too little, but let us not anchor our lives in earthly wealth. If we do, happiness will always be the elusive dream and in fact the impossible dream, because we will be slaves to the temporary and thus inadequate. When wealth becomes our top priority, we are miserable indeed.

OBTAINING EARTHLY WEALTH

Earthly wealth must be obtained in the right way. There can be no "end justifies the means" philosophy for the child of God.

One way we can acquire wealth correctly is to work for it. "Wealth from gambling quickly disappears; wealth from hard work grows" (13:11). "Work brings profit; talk brings poverty!" (14:23).

We are also to reverence and obey God. He will honor such an attitude. "Those who love and follow me [Wisdom] are indeed wealthy. I fill their treasuries" (8:21). "True humility and respect for the Lord lead a man to riches, honor and long life" (22:4). The best way a person can have earthly wealth and be useful with it is to give it to God. We are custodians of his possession. "The earth belongs to God! Everything in all the world is his" (Psalm 24:1). Everything that we are, everything that we have belongs to God! Let's use it for him.

We cannot gain genuine riches through wickedness. "Ill-gotten gain brings no lasting happiness; right living does" (10:2). "Dishonest gain will never last, so why take the risk?" (21:6). We cannot receive genuine wealth by taking advantage of other people. "He who gains by oppressing the poor or by bribing the rich shall end in poverty" (22:16). Likewise, if we try to gain wealth by trying to patronize the rich, God will not bless. When we give to others, it should be out of love and not out of a desire to get something in return.

USING EARTHLY WEALTH PROPERLY

Wealth must be used properly, and that begins with tithing. "Honor the Lord by giving him the first part of all your income, and he will fill your barns with wheat and barley and overflow your wine vats with the finest wines" (3:9, 10). We honor the Lord with our wealth by giving to him first.

All of us will have plenty for our needs if we tithe. All of us can afford to give at least a tithe. The tithe is dramatic proof of our honoring God with our substance. Through it we demonstrate that we belong to him.

God also encourages us to be generous to others. In fact, he instructs us to give for the needs of others. "When you help the poor you are lending to the Lord—and he pays wonderful interest on your loan!" (19:17). God encourages us to be generous with what we have. "It is possible to give away and become richer! It is also possible to hold on too tightly and lose everything. Yes, the liberal man shall be rich! By watering others, he waters himself" (11:24, 25).

We are also instructed to make wise purchases. God is interested in how we spend our money. The virtuous woman is commended because "she goes out to inspect a field, and buys it; with her own hands she plants a vineyard. She is energetic, a hard worker, and watches for bargains. She works far into the night!" (31:16-18). "Only a simpleton believes what he is told! A prudent man checks to see where he is going" (14:15). We should not take everything at face value or believe everything we are told when we get ready to make a purchase. In fact, we need to know what we are paying for before we make that purchase. We should be wise in our investments.

Closely associated with this is the matter of paying debts promptly. One of the greatest blights upon the name of Christ is a child of God who will not pay his bills. "Don't withhold repayment of your debts. Don't say 'some other time,' if you can pay now" (3:27, 28). By paying what we owe, we honor our Lord.

On the other hand, "unless you have the extra cash on hand, don't countersign a note. Why risk everything you own? They'll even take your bed!" (22:26, 27). If we have extra money available, it is all right for us to cosign a note; if we cannot pay it, we shouldn't cosign. God wants us to use our heads about the use of our earthly treasures.

We are also warned to avoid "get rich quick" schemes. "The man who wants to do right will get a rich reward. But the man who wants to get rich quick will quickly fail. Giving preferred treatment to rich people is a clear case of selling one's soul for a piece of bread. Trying to get rich quick is evil and leads to poverty" (28:20-22). These schemes are evil because they are based on a wrong motive. Instead of building on the foundation of love and service, they are based on our own selfishness and greed.

We are also told not to waste our wealth on gluttony and drunkenness (23:19-21). If we overeat or become drunkards, we show that our priorities are out of balance. To exercise such wantonness is to misuse our money.

EARTHLY WEALTH AND REAL RICHES

Earthly wealth is only a small portion of genuine riches. The man who is rich by earthly standards may be poor indeed. He may be wealthy in time but poor by eternal standards. "If you must choose, take a good name rather than great riches; for to be held in loving esteem is better than silver and gold. The rich and the poor are alike before the Lord who made them all" (22:1, 2).

Earthly wealth is a relative thing. Real wealth includes eternal riches which we receive through faith in God. A good name is a greater measure of wealth than possessions. Jesus enlarged upon this when he said, "And I have given you authority over all the power of the Enemy, and to walk among serpents and scorpions and to crush them. Nothing shall injure you! However, the important thing is not that demons obey you, but that your names are registered as citizens of heaven" (Luke 10:19, 20).

Real wealth is not measured by earthly power but by the love in which we are held by our heavenly Father.

The Serpent and the Adder

12

A twenty-three-year-old man I know was hopelessly alcoholic. He reached out desperately for help, but nothing availed. One day he called to say he was ready to kill his father and then take his own life. He had three loaded shotguns at his side. Except for God's intervention, he would have carried out his threat. Alcohol was a tyrant in his life.

How many lives has alcohol ruined? How many lives have been claimed by drunken drivers? How many homes have been broken apart by alcohol?

It would be nice to close our eyes to the problem of alcoholism, but it must be faced. Some say alcohol is only a problem for the old. Not so. According to a Parent-Teacher Association survey, 75 percent of the high school students in the United States drink alcoholic beverages. The tragedy is that 50 percent of heavy high school drinkers become alcoholics. Today the number of teenage alcoholics is greater than the total number of Americans killed in World Wars I and II and in the Korean and Vietnamese conflicts.

Recently a man told me, "If a man wants to be drunk,

he has a right to do it." Does he really? After one glass of beer, a man will take six feet longer to stop his car than otherwise.[1] If my daughter or yours were standing in that six-foot danger zone, then his freedom is our business.

We cannot ignore the alcohol problem. The abuse of alcohol is a crime against society. It costs taxpayers more money than we realize. Alcohol is still the number one drug problem in America. A majority of crimes committed in the United States have some involvement with alcohol and narcotics. Teenagers are now turning from pills, barbituates, and hard narcotics to booze.

It is a severe problem in our society, and the book of Proverbs is not silent on the issue. "Whose heart is filled with anguish and sorrow? Who is always fighting and quarreling? Who is the man with bloodshot eyes and many wounds? It is the one who spends long hours in the taverns, trying out new mixtures. Don't let the sparkle and the smooth taste of strong wine deceive you. For in the end it bites like a poisonous serpent; it stings like an adder" (23:29-32).

CHARACTERISTICS

Proverbs gives some characteristics of alcohol abuse. We don't have to get drunk to find out what they are. God warns us about it because he wants us to enjoy life to its fullest. God never gives a prohibition in order to take the fun out of life. He is the One who puts fun into life. When we are told not to do something, it is for our protection and our health. We parents know about this.

We teach our children to not touch things that are hot because they will be burned. We want to protect them from a burn or the hurt that comes with it. God deals with us in the same way. He knows what destroys life. He knows what takes away our happiness and the possibilities for fulfillment.

The main reason God gives such clear warning about the matter of alcohol lies in the very nature of man. Our ability to love, understand, and be intelligent is due to our being made in the image of God. Alcohol affects our ability to be rational, impairs our relationship with God.

Proverbs warns rulers about using alcohol. "And it is not for kings, O Lemuel, to drink wine and whiskey" (31:4). That seems unfair to many of us. It seems as if someone should be able to drink whatever he wants if he is a ruler. Why not? "For if they drink they may forget their duties and be unable to give justice to those who are oppressed" (31:5).

Alcohol breeds irresponsibility. A ruler who drinks alcohol does not have the intelligence, the ability, the discipline to administer law correctly. When he remembers the law, he perverts it.

Ineptness is another characteristic of those who use alcohol. "Hard liquor is for sick men at the brink of death, and wine for those in deep depression" (31:6). There were no sedatives in Bible times as we know them. Alcohol was used for medicinal purposes, and is today. There are some valid uses for alcohol, but misuse dulls the senses. Many people use alcohol and narcotics in their search for purposeful living. There is no life in this abuse, only dullness and ineptitude. It causes us to be insensitive to life and to those around us. That is why we are told, "And afterwards you will say, 'I didn't even know it when they beat me up.... Let's go and have another drink!' " (23:35).

A person who drinks will do crazy, foolish things. "You will see hallucinations and have delirium tremens, and you will say foolish, silly things that would embarrass you no end when sober. You will stagger like a sailor tossed at sea, clinging to a swaying mast" (23:33, 34). He clings to anything that will keep him from being washed overboard. That's OK in the middle of the sea, but in the middle of the street? Have you ever seen a drunk person face a curb on his hands and knees because that curb looked six feet tall? What folly!

Drinkers sometimes claim, "Drinking brings out the real 'me!' " Truthfully, we do not want to know the real "me." The Bible declares that the real "me" is bound for hell, being a sinner by nature, by choice, by conduct. If allowed to take over, the real "me" will embarrass us, make fools out of us, and destroy us. Rather, we need to let God transform us. We need to let God be released in us, so he can be himself in us.

The user of alcohol sees unreal and strange things. "You will see hallucinations and have delirium tremens" (23:33). The person who uses alcohol to excess sees things that are not there, the unreal. He is removed from reality; his senses are distorted and dulled. God has given to us a wonderful world in which to live. The drunkard isn't able to enjoy it.

Despair is the ultimate end of the use of alcohol, a

despair filled with anguish and sorrow. "Whose heart is filled with anguish and sorrow? Who is always fighting and quarreling? Who is the man with bloodshot eyes and many wounds? It is the one who spends long hours in the taverns, trying out new mixtures. Don't let the sparkle and smooth taste of strong wine deceive you. For in the end it bites like a poisonous serpent; it stings like an adder" (23:29-32). The phrase "trying out new mixtures" refers to experimenting with new ways to mix drinks. We live in the day of an ever-increasing variety of mixed drinks. They lead to sorrow, anguish, contention, babbling.

Despair brings sorrow and anguish. The heavy drinker has a heavy heart. He is unhappy with himself and turns to alcohol to escape from himself, an impossibility.

The drinker of alcohol is always fighting and quarreling. His life is always filled with turmoil. "Wine gives false courage; hard liquor leads to brawls; what fools men are to let it master them, making them reel drunkenly down the street!" (20:1). The term "false courage" comes from the Hebrew word translated "mocker" in Proverbs 19:29: "Mockers and rebels shall be severely punished." False courage is foolish courage. Is it wrong to be afraid to step in front of traffic? Certainly not. But people under the influence of alcohol sometimes lack healthy fear and so become victims of death, destruction, and despair.

The ultimate end for most people who abuse alcohol is poverty. "A man who loves pleasure becomes poor; wine and luxury are not the way to riches!" (21:17). Not only does the man who drinks end up poor materially, but he also misses out on the riches of a Christ-filled life.

CONCLUSION

What is the impact of the use of alcohol in our lives? Where does it lead? Some say, "I just drink on social occasions. I have a little wine with my meals." Proverbs retorts, "Don't let the sparkle and smooth taste of strong wine deceive you. For in the end it bites like a poisonous serpent; it stings like an adder" (23:31, 32).

Alcohol can master us, control us. People say, "I can take it or leave it." But have you noticed that they always take it and never leave it? The writer of Proverbs tells of a man who became so drunk he got sick and didn't know it. He was beaten severely and didn't know it until he sobered up. What was his reaction when he woke up? "Let's go and have another drink!" (23:35). He was blinded by alcohol, and any man in darkness is easily mastered.

A frog cannot be killed merely by dropping it into a pot of boiling water. He would immediately feel the danger and leap out of the pot. But if you put him in warm water and heat it very slowly, he will soon be cooked, unaware of what is happening to him.

We may say, "We don't want drunks rampaging on the streets. We don't want narcotics legalized. We would never tolerate such things." But little by little, by our permissiveness and our complacency, we have been cooked in our own pleasure and foolishness.

Nine million people are alcoholics or are dependent on alcohol in America today. Sixty-five percent of American adults drink![2] Five of every fifteen people in America who start drinking alcohol become dependent upon it. Three of those five become alcoholics, and the two others have serious problems because of their drinking.[3] In addition, there are untold thousands of children who are innocent victims of alcohol. Nearly 90 percent of children in children's homes across America are not orphans.[4] They are not there because they have no parents, but because their parents cannot or will not care for them. Too many of these parents have a drinking problem.

Alcohol "bites like a poisonous serpent; it stings like an adder" (23:32). The final end of alcohol is death. The nondrinker lives a longer—and more meaningful—life than do those who abuse alcohol.

In the United States alone, some 15,000 people die from alcoholism every year. In fact, only three diseases kill more people than alcohol—tuberculosis, cancer, and heart ailments. If we add deaths that are triggered by alcohol (automobile accidents, crime, etc.), alcohol becomes the number one killer in the United States today.[5]

I personally do not believe we can call alcoholism a disease—certainly not in the same sense as cancer, heart disease, multiple sclerosis, or tuberculosis. Instead of curing alcoholism, we permit the liquor industry to spend incredible amounts of money advertising its products, products that bring death.

CURE

God's Word tells us of the cure of alcoholism—a spiritual cure, because alcoholism is the result of sin.

Why do people drink? Because they are guilty. They want to forget. Something has happened in their lives and they want to get away from it. Or because they are bored. They have no purpose or direction in life. Or because they are angry—at life, their parents, their families, their friends, or their employers.

Nothing is so characteristic of American society as revolutionaries who say, "All we want to do is destroy. We have no alternative but to tear down." People who resort to alcohol often have that kind of anger, resentment, hatred, fear. Their problem in a word is sin.

Jesus Christ came to be the cure for sin, to free us from the oppression, slavery, pain, death that sin causes. Alcoholism is just one of the many symptoms of sin. "Trust the Lord completely; don't ever trust yourself. In everything you do, put God first, and he will direct you and crown your efforts with success" (3:5, 6). Our own understanding will lead us astray, but God can guide us into life.

"They say that what is right is wrong, and what is wrong is right; that black is white and white is black; bitter is sweet and sweet is bitter" (Isaiah 5:20). That is what the liquor industry does. They call evil good and give darkness instead of light. They give bitterness instead of sweetness. "Woe to those who are wise and shrewd in their own eyes!" (Isaiah 5:21). The writer of Proverbs agrees. If we trust ourselves or lean on our own intelligence and understanding, we will go astray.

If we try to figure life out for ourselves, if we try to find a solution to the pressure under which we live, if we try to find a direction for life on our own, we will fail.

Jesus Christ can banish our guilt with forgiveness. He can give us new life. He can take away the anger of our hearts and flood our souls with peace and comfort. He can take away the hatred and bitterness and resentment and bring back love. He can take away boredom and give us a direction that is exciting.

God is up to something great and that is why Jesus Christ came. He wants to include us in his wonderful plans. Christ is the answer to our need. It is not to be found in drugs or alcohol. The cure is to find life in Jesus Christ. As we bow our knees before him, he will empower us to be what he wants us to be and to do what he wants us to do. God wants our hearts to be open and yielded to him. Through us he can change the world.

NOTES

1. Wayne Dehoney, *Challenges to the Cross* (Nashville: Broadman Press, 1962), p. 53.

2. Albert Q. Maisel, "Alcohol and Your Brain," *The Reader's Digest*, June 1970.

3. Dehoney, p. 51.

4. Dehoney, p. 55.

5. *Commercial Appeal* (Memphis) April 3, 1960, p. 14. Quoted in Dehoney, *Challenges to the Cross*.

The Value of Public Worship

The natural result of the kind of life that is described in Proverbs is a public avowal, a public commitment, a public worship of the Lord.

If we are to live as God wants us to it must be in his wisdom. Such a life will demonstrate the purpose and goal of God in our lives. We are to reverence the Lord, praise him, honor him. If we are to do that, we cannot do it quietly, we cannot do it privately, we cannot do it alone. Genuine honor to God must be seen. It must be shared. "Honor the Lord by giving him the first part of all your income, and he will fill your barns with wheat and barley and overflow your wine vats with the finest wines" (3:9, 10). By our giving to the Lord, we honor him. It is an act of public dedication, public commitment.

PUBLIC WORSHIP AND PRIVATE WORSHIP
Sometimes people say, "I love God, but I can worship him by myself." Or, "I can worship God in a boat on

the lake with a fishing pole in my hand just as well as I can at church." But private worship will always result in public worship. The testimony of the Word of God and the glad witness of our hearts is that when we have entered into a private worship with God, we will give evidence of it publicly. We need to share with one another and draw upon each other's strength as we worship and serve the Lord together.

The New Testament calls the gatherings of believers a "fellowship," *koinonia*. It is a time to bear one another's burdens and to lift up one another. Our hearts are encouraged as we sing. Our souls are elevated as we are led in prayer and pray. Our hearts are uplifted by the Word of God as it is proclaimed. Participation in public worship gives evidence that something is happening to us in private.

Throughout Proverbs we are shown that loving and serving God is a way of life for God's children. "Yes, if you want better insight and discernment, and are searching for them as you would for lost money or hidden treasure, then wisdom will be given you, and knowledge of God himself; you will soon learn the importance of reverence for the Lord and of trusting him" (2:3-5). If we have that kind of craving for godly living, it will express itself. Such commitment will show.

"Keep these thoughts ever in mind; let them penetrate deep within your heart, for they will mean real life for you, and radiant health" (4:21-23). If Christ is real to us, if God is worshiped in our souls, it will be demonstrated in our lives. Public worship and service is the natural result of private commitment.

ABUSING PUBLIC WORSHIP

In the book of Proverbs God gives us some very stern warnings about the abuse of worship.

A wicked person may use public worship as a means of obtaining personal gain or achieving a personal goal. Because he has no commitment to God, his worship is unacceptable to God. Take as an example the harlot making her pitch to a potential lover. As she caresses his face and kisses his cheeks, she says, "I have peace offerings with me; this day have I paid my vows" (7:14, KJV). Most scholars concur that she had been to the Temple to make her sacrifice earlier in the day. She had already performed her religious duty of worship and had enough left over from the sacrifice to take with her as she carried out her godless activities. This was a malicious misuse of worship, for "God loathes the gifts of evil men, especially if they are trying to bribe him!" (21:27). "The Lord hates the gifts of the wicked, but delights in the prayers of his people" (15:8). The gifts of the wicked are an abomination to God because they are bribes, an abuse of worship. We should search our hearts when we come to worship, to be sure that we are not coming to the house of the Lord for selfish purposes.

We must also beware of hypocrisy—pretending we are devoted, compassionate, committed children of God when we are not. "We can justify our every deed but God looks at our motives. God is more pleased when we are just and fair than when we give him gifts" (21:2, 3). God is more pleased when we share his character than when we look pious. God says, "If you are going to worship me publicly, live your profession. Put it into practice. Be the kind of person you seem to be when you worship."

None of us is actually what we appear to be. But the writer of Proverbs is dealing with deliberate deception of those with whom we worship. In Acts 5 we see such deception in the lives of Ananias and Sapphira. They were Christians, they were part of the church, but they abused worship. They pretended to be something that they were not, pretending to offer something they did not offer. By their hypocrisy, they lied to others and worse, lied to God. They were struck dead because of their hypocrisy.

HONORING GOD

Public worship honors God, because it is public witness of our faith. Amazingly, if some celebrity is going to sing over the Labor Day weekend in a cotton patch in West Texas, 150,000 people show up. They even come a day early and sleep on the ground to be a part of the occasion. They give public witness of some type of commitment.

God wants us to come together to worship him and to demonstrate our faith publicly, because this honors him. As God's people, we can't make an impact on the world unless we work together. Even when it seems we are not noticed or that nothing will come of it, we need to honor God with our public worship.

Why does this honor God? Because it delights him. It is a joy to him. "I bless the holy name of God with all my heart. Yes, I will bless the Lord and not forget the glorious things he does for me" (Psalm 103:1, 2). "The Lord hates the gifts of the wicked, but delights in the prayers of his people" (15:8). "The Lord is far from the wicked, but he hears the prayers of the righteous" (15:29). It delights God to hear his people pray. He enjoys moving among us in miraculous power.

Our public worship can reveal God to other people, can help them see God at work. We show God to the world when we put him first. "If you want favor with both God and man, and a reputation for good judgment and common sense, then trust the Lord completely; don't ever trust yourself. In everything you do, put God first, and he will direct you and crown your efforts with success" (3:4-6). When we truly worship God in our souls and trust him with all our hearts, when we acknowledge him and honor him in our worship together, we tell the world that our lives are not to be explained by human understanding alone. We are responsible to reveal God's truth to the world.

Public worship reveals our true allegiance, our commitment to God. It shows what we are in our hearts. "For God is closely watching you, and he weighs carefully everything you do" (5:21). Worshiping the Lord together reminds us that God sees our lives, that he knows our needs, that he knows our sins and deals with them. As we worship together, we have the opportunity to again tell God we love him and will faithfully serve him.

When we worship God together, we tear away the false barriers that separate us from one another. "The rich and the poor are alike before the Lord who made them all" (22:2). "Rich and poor are alike in this: each depends on God for light" (29:13). When we meet together, a man's true value is seen. There are no rich or poor before God—we are all alike. We all have the same access to God—through Jesus Christ. No one can buy his way into the kingdom of God. No one can push or boast his way into the kingdom. When we worship publicly, we give a beautiful witness and testimony that honors God. We all stand equal before him. Whether we are rich or poor, when we stand before God we are all aware of our sinfulness, our nothingness. We cannot make it apart from God's grace. We are compelled to cry out, "O God, how could you love me?"

Public worship strips away the veneer of earthly status and class. In those moments, we stand at the greatest opportunity of life. We stand together before God. There God can deal with our hearts on an equal basis regardless of our age, race, means, or status. When we publicly worship God, we honor him. And he rewards those who honor him.

14

The Power of a Word

We give too little thought to the things we say. Are they good or evil? Are they words of animosity or love? The book of Proverbs reminds us again and again that if we are wise, we are careful about our words.

A man's character is revealed by what he says. A fool expresses his wrath by his speaking; a prudent man covers his shame by not speaking. We must be careful about our language. "A good man is known by his truthfulness; a false man by deceit and lies. Some people like to make cutting remarks, but the words of the wise soothe and heal. Truth stands the test of time; lies are soon exposed" (12:17-19).

The writer of Proverbs listed seven things that God hates (6:16-19), and three of them had to do with the things we say.

THE PERSUASION OF WORDS

Words are compelling. They have great impact for good

or ill. They can crush a person's feelings. A thoughtless word can devastate one's life. There are some people who can say a word and they might as well pierce you through with a sword. "Some people like to make cutting remarks" (12:18). "What dainty morsels rumors are. They are eaten with great relish!... A man's courage can sustain his broken body, but when courage dies, what hope is left?" (18:8, 14). How difficult it is to endure (let alone triumph) when our courage dies and we are crushed by cruel words.

There is another side of the coin—words can encourage and uplift us. "The words of the wise soothe and heal" (12:18). "Anxious hearts are very heavy but a word of encouragement does wonders!" (12:25).

We live in a world where we are thrown together with others constantly. We must often speak to one another. Sometimes we speak well and at other times we speak ill to one another. It would be wonderful if we determined to watch our words, be nice to one another—if we would speak encouraging words instead of finding ways to cut someone off, put someone down, discourage someone, or otherwise affront one another. We should use words to uplift and encourage instead of crush and hurt others.

Dr. Jeff Ray of Southwestern Baptist Theological Seminary used to say to young preachers, "Boys, be nice to everybody because everybody's having a hard time." That would be good for us to remember. Other people have feelings, other people need encouragement. They don't need to be crushed. They need to be built up. Our words can help.

Throughout Proverbs we are told that words determine attitudes. And attitudes can destroy a friendship.
"Idle hands are the devil's workshop; idle lips are his
mouthpiece. An evil man sows strife; gossip separates
the best of friends" (16:27, 28). A person who whispers
or speaks badly about others can set his hearers against
them. We are prone to believe absurd things about
others simply because they are told to us. It is amazing
how misinformed we sometimes are about others.
Often we have to readjust our opinion when we get to
know them because of wrong pictures we had of them.
Our attitudes are often set toward people before we
ever meet them, because of the power and persuasion
of words.

By words we can inflate our own self-esteem out of its
proper perspective. We are too easily flattered. "Flattery is a trap; evil men are caught in it, but good men
stay away and sing for joy" (29:5, 6). We need to be
careful of those who would flatter us. We must also be
careful of those who would condemn us. We are un-
doubtedly not nearly so good as our admirers think, nor
as bad as our critics suggest. Our self-esteem can be
blown out of proportion.

Words are persuasive. They can cause us to believe
some things about ourselves and others that are not
true. In addition, we must be careful of the words that
we put into our own minds. Words have a way of forming and shaping our beliefs and attitudes. They even
shape our faith. We need to be careful of the things we
read and hear because of their persuasive power over
us.

THE PENETRATION OF WORDS

Words have a way of spreading like a fire to penetrate the very depths of our being, for good or for evil. "Love forgets mistakes; nagging about them parts the best of friends" (17:9). "To hate is to be a liar; to slander is to be a fool" (10:18).

Words have amazing penetrating power. Unfortunately, some of the worst slanders come from the lips of people who ought to know better. Shakespeare put these words in the mouth of Iago:

> *Good name in man, and woman, dear my lord,*
> *Is the immediate jewel of our souls.*
> *Who steals my purse steals trash; tis something,*
>   *nothing;*
> *'Twas mine, 'tis his, and has been slave to thousands.*
> *But he that filches from me my good name,*
> *Robs me of that which not enriches him and makes me*
>   *poor indeed.*

(Othello, Act III, Scene 3, lines 155-161).

Slander is gossip. It has no basis in fact. It is the repetition of something that is not true or even something that is half true, giving a false impression.

In the words of the *Talmud*, "The slanderous tongue kills three: the slandered, the slanderer, and him who listens to the slander."

THE PROBLEM WITH WORDS

Words can never be a substitute for deeds. We can never make up what we lack in living and being with our talk. "Work brings profit; talk brings poverty!" (14:23). We must do more than talk. Anybody can say, "Look at me—what a wonderful Christian I am," but he must also put his faith into action.

Words cannot alter the facts. "Pretty words may hide a wicked heart, just as a pretty glaze covers a common clay pot. A man with hate in his heart may sound pleasant enough, but don't believe him; for he is cursing you in his heart. Though he pretends to be so kind, his hatred will finally come to light for all to see. The man who sets a trap for others will get caught in it himself. Roll a boulder down on someone, and it will roll back and crush you. Flattery is a form of hatred and wounds cruelly" (26:23-28). Denying a wrong does not make it right. "Don't try to disclaim responsibility by saying you didn't know about it. For God, who knows all hearts, knows yours, and he knows you knew! And he will reward everyone according to his deeds" (24:12). God knows the truth. Our words cannot change the facts.

We may talk a wonderful game when it comes to being a Christian. But if we do not know Jesus Christ personally as our Savior, all the words we've spoken from the time of our birth until we stand before God will not help—we are lost. If there is wickedness and sin in our lives, we cannot change it simply by telling people that it's not so. For instance, we read, "A man who robs his parents and says, 'What's wrong with that?' is no better than a murderer" (28:24). No matter how much this man claims he is only taking what is his, he has indeed committed evil.

Words, whether good or evil, cannot compel us to respond to them. "Sometimes mere words are not enough—discipline is needed. For the words may not be heeded" (29:19). We cannot make someone respond a certain way merely using the right words. And words alone can never force us to do evil—we choose to do it. "And remember, when someone wants to do wrong it is never God who is tempting him, for God never wants to do wrong and never tempts anyone else to do it. Temptation is the pull of man's own evil thoughts and wishes" (James 1:13, 14). Each of us is his own biggest problem. We have only ourselves to blame when we sin. Of course, the most eloquent words in the world cannot make us better persons either. We choose our own response.

THE PREPARATION OF WORDS

We should want good words, helpful words to come from our lips. If this is our desire, we must work diligently to make it come to pass. It doesn't happen naturally.

As we prepare to use the right kind of words, we must know God's ideals about the matter. In the first place, our words should always be honest. "Truth stands the test of time; lies are soon exposed. Deceit fills hearts that are plotting for evil; joy fills hearts that are planning for good!" (12:19, 20). "God delights in those who keep their promises, and abhors those who don't" (12:22).

In addition to being honest, our words should be

carefully chosen. "The man of few words and settled
mind is wise; therefore, even a fool is thought to be
wise when he is silent. It pays him to keep his mouth
shut" (17:27, 28). "Don't talk so much. You keep putting your foot in your mouth. Be sensible and turn off
the flow! When a good man speaks, he is worth listening to, but the words of fools are a dime a dozen. A
godly man gives good advice, but a rebel is destroyed
by lack of common sense" (10:19-21). If we talk long
enough and fast enough and say enough, we will prob-
ably get into trouble. My mother used to tell me, "Son,
you aren't learning anything while you are talking."
Someone has said, "It is better to keep quiet and let
everyone think you are a fool than to open your mouth
and prove it."

Another prerequisite for wise words is calmness. We
should never speak in anger. "A soft answer turns away
wrath, but harsh words cause quarrels. A wise teacher
makes learning a joy; a rebellious teacher spouts
foolishness. The Lord is watching everywhere and
keeps his eye on both the evil and the good. Gentle
words cause life and health; griping brings discouragement. Only a fool despises his father's advice; a
wise son considers each suggestion" (15:1-5).

The writer of Proverbs gives us three reasons why we
should use calm words. First, it gives our tempers a
chance to cool down before we speak. If we respond
with anger, our words are usually wrong, clumsy, abu-
sive, or hurtful. Also, calm words give us a chance to
hear both sides of the matter before taking action.
"What a shame—yes, how stupid!—to decide before

knowing the facts!'' (18:13). Too many people make up their minds before they hear the facts. They act on incomplete or distorted information, and their words pour out like a torrent as they pass on information or gossip.

A third reason we should use calm words is that they can have a great healing effect. A person who waits carefully and weighs his language and his words will have power when he speaks. "Be patient and you will finally win, for a soft tongue can break hard bones" (25:15).

Our words should be appropriate. "Timely advice is as lovely as golden apples in a silver basket. It is a badge of honor to accept valid criticism. A faithful employee is as refreshing as a cool day in the hot summertime. One who doesn't give the gift he promised is like a cloud blowing over a desert without dropping any rain. Be patient and you will finally win, for a soft tongue can break hard bones" (25:11-15).

The Apostle James tells us that the tongue cannot be tamed. He calls it an unruly fire, a poison, the most difficult part of man to control (James 3:2-10). Our tongues cause us much sorrow, bitterness, and trouble. We need God's help if we are to produce wise words.

"A good man thinks before he speaks; the evil man pours out his evil words without a thought" (15:28). If we want to use the kind of words God would have us use, words that bring help and wholeness to others, words that encourage fellowship, then we need to consider our words before we utter them. Our words tell others what we are. Someone may have a bad habit of cursing. That is what is inside him. Another may often lose his temper. That is the kind of person he is. We may be critical and contentious. If so, it is because of what we are in our spirit. Our words come out of our hearts and reflect the real us, just as the Word Jesus Christ is the perfect reflection of God.

When we face God, we drop to our knees and say, "O God, like Isaiah in the temple, I am a man of unclean lips and I dwell in the midst of a people of unclean lips." How desperately we need the experience of Isaiah in our own lives. We need the angel of God to come and touch our lips as he says, "Your sins are all forgiven" (Isaiah 6:6,7). Why did the angel touch Isaiah's lips? Because with his lips he confessed that he was a sinner, that had offended God, had rebelled against God, and had said things that should not be spoken. From that time Isaiah became one of the greatest prophets of God.

We too need to come before the Lord and realize that our words are a reflection of what we are. Our careless, rebellious, critical, and blasphemous words keep us from experiencing God's power in our lives. When he touches our hearts, our words will change, because we will change.

Jesus Christ came to change what we are. We need not despair because our words reveal us to be sinners. Jesus Christ can and will change us if we turn to him in repentance and faith. That is his invitation. If we let him come into our lives and change us, our words can be what they ought to be—words of wisdom that reflect the power of God in our lives.

The Beauty of Friendship

15

"A true friend is always loyal, and a brother is born to help in time of need" (17:17). In the depths of our darkest moments, we discover our strongest ties of friendship. In those situations we discover a brother, a friend, someone who will stand with us.

If Christian people were friends to one another, we could win the world to Christ. People would be knocking on our doors wanting to be part of such community. Sadly, we don't like one another, we don't get along with each other, we don't behave like friends. And we act the same way toward those who are lost. As a result, our evangelistic efforts lag behind the world's population growth. This is the opposite of the expressed intention of our Lord: "And so I am giving a new commandment to you now—love each other just as much as I love you. Your strong love for each other will prove to the world that you are my disciples" (John 13:34, 35).

This is the acid test of our discipleship. Men know that we belong to Jesus when they see our love, our friendship. That is the bond between Christians. Our Lord said, "I demand that you love each other as much as I love you. And here is how to measure it—the greatest love is shown when a person lays down his life for his friend; and you are my friends if you obey me. I no longer call you slaves, for a master doesn't confide in his slaves; now you are my friends, proved by the fact that I have told you everything the Father told me" (John 15:12-15). Friendship offers us a great opportunity to win the world to Christ. When we act toward each other in love and respond to one another as friends, we teach the world about the love of Christ.

Friendship must be nurtured, cared for, protected. The Hebrew word *alluph*, meaning "friend" or "leader," appears several times in Proverbs, and is also translated "guide" and "neighbor." The statement concerning the sinful woman and her problems in 2:17 uses *alluph* and indicates that the reason the sinful woman is such is because she has forsaken her "guide" (KJV), referring to her husband. She has turned her back on her friend.

The Psalms tell us very clearly about the betrayal of friendship. "It was not an enemy who taunted me— then I could have borne it; I could have hidden and escaped. But it was you, a man like myself, my companion and my friend. What fellowship we had, what wonderful discussions as we walked together to the Temple of the Lord on holy days" (Psalm 55:12-14). "Even my best friend has turned against me—a man I completely trusted; how often we ate together" (Psalm 41:9).

"An evil man sows strife; gossip separates the best of friends" (16:28). We expect viciousness from our enemies, but not from our friends. We cannot be betrayed by an enemy, but by a friend. We must guard our friendships against all threats.

The writer of Proverbs also gives us some warnings about making friendships. "Keep away from angry, short-tempered men, lest you learn to be like them and endanger your soul" (22:24, 25). The angry person has no self-control, no self-discipline. We are warned not to make friends with those who have characteristics that we do not want. If we do, we will learn his ways and trap our own souls. We will step into the same pitfalls our friend fell into.

LOYALTY

True friendship is based on loyalty, a loyalty that expresses itself in faithfulness.

"A true friend is always loyal, and a brother is born to help in time of need" (17:17). A friend sticks with us when the going gets rough. He is always there. He will not turn his back on us. "There are 'friends' who pretend to be friends, but there is a friend who sticks closer than a brother" (18:24). Robert South says, "A friend will play the role of an advocate before he assumes the role of a judge." A friend will faithfully stand by us through thick and thin.

"Putting confidence in an unreliable man is like chewing with a sore tooth, or trying to run on a broken foot" (25:19). This man is worthless to our need, reliable in his loyalty.

A second thing that reveals the beauty of friendship

is honesty. There are many so-called friends, false friends, who will betray our relationship by telling us things that are not true. A real friend is open and honest with us. "Open rebuke is better than hidden love! Wounds from a friend are better than kisses from an enemy!" (27:5, 6). A real friend tells us the truth, even when it hurts. An enemy, like Judas, will knock himself out giving dramatic demonstrations of his loyalty, and at the same time try to cut our throats.

A true friend will tell us the truth in love. "In the end, people appreciate frankness more than flattery" (28:23). Sometimes even friends do not appreciate the truth at the time it is presented. Nevertheless, when all is said and done, they will see the benefit of it and thank us for being truthful.

Another aspect of loyalty is suffering. "Love forgets mistakes; nagging about them parts the best of friends" (17:9). When a friend hurts us, whether inadvertently or deliberately, we should suffer in silence rather than retaliate. To strike back would be a betrayal of our friendship.

There are times when friendship requires us not to say something that we're sure is true. "I don't gossip— it's all true," we say. True or not, it is not right for us to say anything that harms others. We need to weigh the impact of our words before we speak.

LOVE

Friendship is also based on love. One of the most beautiful expressions of that kind of love is seen in the narrative about David and Jonathan. "After King Saul had finished his conversation with David, David met Jonathan, the king's son, and there was an immediate bond of love between them. Jonathan swore to be his blood brother" (1 Samuel 18:1-3). The King James Version says, "Jonathan loved him as his own soul."

That kind of love, the heart of genuine friendship, involves fellowship. "There are 'friends' who pretend to be friends, but there is a friend who sticks closer than a brother" (18:24). Friends spend much time together. They need each other. They enjoy each other. We were not made for isolation or solitary living. We were made to fellowship.

The other day someone brought me a newspaper clipping, picturing a man sitting forlorn and alone on a park bench. A caption simply read, "Solitude." Underneath the picture the text said, "Solitude can be a blessed relief from a hectic day, or endless hours of agony for those who find themselves constantly alone. There are times when being alone is a comfort, but loneliness is never comforting, and being forgotten can only bring despair." We need one another.

Love also includes kindness. "He that loveth pureness of heart, for the grace of his lips the king shall be his friend" (22:11, KJV). We ought to share gracious, kind words with one another. We ought to care about one another's feelings. "If you shout a pleasant greeting to a friend too early in the morning, he will count it as a curse!" (27:14). We may make a mockery of friendship by making exaggerated public displays of affection to someone. In fact, that very display may become a tool of malice and pervert the course of a friendship. "A man that hath friends must show himself friendly" (18:24, KJV). This is the kindness of true Christian love.

There are few things in this world more beautiful than real friendship, which is based upon and demonstrates itself in genuine love, a love that does not depend on reciprocation. It is a love for an individual because of the individual himself. Regardless of circumstances, in real friendship there is a constant love and loyalty.

The genuine beauty of friendship is seen when that kind of love is returned and shared. We love each other, not because of what we are, but in spite of what we are. We love each other, not because we deserve such love and friendship, but because we need such love and friendship. As we express this kind of friendship, we discover the delights and the joy and the deep sense of satisfaction that such friendship brings. How beautiful friendship is!

The Most Dangerous Man in Town

16

In the book of Proverbs we meet a man who is given at least four different names. He is called "simple," "mocker," "rebel"; but more predominantly, he is called "fool." One thing is clear concerning this person—he is a menace to society, his friends, and God's people. He is the most dangerous person in town.

He is not a fool because he is silly or stupid, but because certain characteristics in his life work against him rather than for him. These characteristics cause him to be a heartache rather than a blessing to others. He may have wonderful mental capacities, but he deliberately refuses to use them. Such a choice makes him dangerous to others. As a result, we need to be able to identify him and mark him well.

CHARACTERISTICS

What makes the fool dangerous? He takes sin lightly. To him sin is a toy, a plaything, not something to be taken seriously. "If a man enjoys folly, something is wrong! The sensible stay on the pathways of right"

(15:21). Sinfulness and foolishness are fun to the fool.
They delight him even though they work for his defeat
and against his happiness. The fool does not stop to
consider the consequences of his actions. He does not
think about the hurt his words bring. He is not concerned about what sin does to him or others. A man
who takes sin lightly refuses to believe that the ultimate
end of sin is death. Such a man is a fool.

Through the words of Wisdom we learn more about
the fool. " 'You simpletons!' she cries. 'How long will
you go on being fools? How long will you scoff at wisdom and fight the facts?... For you turned away from
me—to death; your own complacency will kill you.
Fools! But all who listen to me shall live in peace and
safety, unafraid' " (1:22, 32, 33). It is folly to treat sin so
lightly, but the fool does just that. "As a dog returns to
his vomit, so a fool repeats his folly" (26:11). Can you
think of anything more disgusting than that?

The fool also has a closed mind. We need not bother
him with facts, he makes up his mind without them. "I
was looking out the window of my house one day, and
saw a simple-minded lad, a young man lacking common sense" (7:6, 7). The fool has his own version of the
truth. "A wise teacher makes learning a joy; a rebellious teacher spouts foolishness" (15:2). The fool closes
his mind to the truth. He has his own peculiar way of
looking at life. He will do things his own way.

The fool is naive. Naivete is not necessarily a bad
trait. The fool, however, is naive to the extreme. He
flirts with temptations without regard to their danger to
him. He oftens skirts the edge of indiscretion. The fool

trusts everyone around him without distinction. He accepts everything at face value. He is naive, simple, a fool who does not investigate the facts. As a result, he is easily led into sin and folly. He passes along the street in the twilight of the evening, knowing he will possibly commit immorality. When he comes upon a wayward girl, she seduces him with "her pretty speech, her coaxing and her wheedling, until he yielded to her. He couldn't resist her flattery" (7:21).

The fool is so naive that he becomes a victim of his own simplicity. Anyone who will permit himself to be placed in a position of potential sin and not protect himself is a fool. Even as Christians, we can be so naive that we fall victim to the worse kind of deceit and sin. There is not a sin that we cannot commit if left to our own resources. We need godly protection or we will surely fall. The fool says, "I do not need it" and soon becomes a victim of Satan.

The fool deliberately and maliciously causes trouble. In contrast to the wise man, the fool's approach to problems is quarrelsome. "A soft answer turns away wrath, but harsh words cause quarrels" (15:1). "Throw out the mocker, and you will be rid of tension, fighting and quarrels" (22:10). Contention and strife make up the fool's mode of operation.

The fool is incredibly fickle. He will say one thing today and something else tomorrow. He will believe one thing today and something else next week. He is unreliable and has no sense of direction in life. "Wisdom is the main pursuit of sensible men, but a fool's goals are at the ends of the earth!" (17:24). A man who gives himself to God has the light of God in his heart. As a result, his mind and will have access to the wisdom of God. God's wisdom gives us direction, but the eyes of a fool are at the ends of the earth. He never stays put, never looks in the same place twice. He is always looking around, searching for happiness and purpose. He looks here and there, up and down, on and off, yes and no, but never finds satisfaction. He is a fool.

The fool will never admit he is wrong. "A rebuke to a man of common sense is more effective than a hundred lashes on the back of a rebel" (17:10). The fool is a fanatic with no common sense. He is determined to do what he wants whether it is right or wrong. He never learns from others, or from his own mistakes (he doesn't make any!). "It is safer to meet a bear robbed of her cubs than a fool caught in his folly" (17:12). The fool makes up his mind to do something and cannot be dissuaded. He is always right and everyone else is wrong. If he loses his sense of direction, he merely doubles his efforts in order to gain his objective. "The wise man looks ahead. The fool attempts to fool himself and won't face facts" (14:8). The fool deceives himself and others. He cannot be depended upon or trusted. He is a fool.

A fool brings grief to his parents and refuses to listen to them. "Only a fool despises his father's advice; a wise son considers each suggestion" (15:5). "It's no fun to be a rebel's father.... A rebellious son is a grief to his father and a bitter blow to his mother" (17:21, 25). The fool is a rebellious son (or daughter) who causes nothing but heartache for his father.

COUNSEL

God tells us to avoid the fool, to stay away from him. "He that walketh with wise men shall be wise; but a companion of fools shall be destroyed" (13:20, KJV). The man whose inner circle of friends is composed of fools will become a fool himself. That is why we must avoid close friendships and associations with fools. Furthermore, "to trust a rebel to convey a message is as foolish as cutting off your feet and drinking poison!" (26:6). When we rely on a fool to carry out our communications, we invite disaster to pay a visit. Don't associate with a fool.

CONCLUSION

"The curse of God is on the wicked, but his blessing is on the upright. The Lord mocks at mockers, but helps the humble" (3:33, 34). The fool sows strife, bitterness, despair, and destruction, and he will reap what he sows. "Don't be misled; remember that you can't ignore God and get away with it: a man will always reap just the kind of crop he sows! If he sows to please his own wrong desires, he will be planting seeds of evil and he will surely reap a harvest of spiritual decay and death; but if he plants the good things of the Spirit, he will reap the everlasting life which the Holy Spirit gives him" (Galatians 6:7, 8). If we sow rebellion against God, we will reap the wrath of God upon our lives. God mocks the mockers.

Don't be a fool, a scorner, a scoffer. When we give

our lives to Christ, he puts his Spirit in us. He gives us a life that is happy and full. A fool cannot grasp that, so he scoffs and scorns God. His eyes run to and fro through the earth and never settle on the purpose of life. We need not be like the fool. The child of God can find understanding, can experience God's purpose and happiness in this life. He can do that by responding to the love of God through faith in Jesus Christ.

The Quarrelsome Heart

17

Proverbs is a very personal and practical book. As such, it can be very distressing to us. Its quest for us is that we may know wisdom, the skill to live a beautiful life. Its admonitions and teachings reach into our hearts and probe them to show us how to know ourselves. If we are to please God, we must understand what Proverbs says about our hearts.

For one thing, Proverbs talks about the quarrelsome heart. Such a heart may to all outward appearances seem happy and peaceful. Not so. In every foolish person's heart, there is war. "It is an honor for a man to stay out of a fight. Only fools insist on quarreling" (20:3). This quarrelsome spirit may or may not express itself to others in ordinary circumstances, but in times of stress it certainly shows itself. Fellowship between brethren is often disrupted because of a heart looking for a fight.

Quarrelsomeness is a problem of the heart. It indicates that the individual is not at peace with God. Because God is not the author of confusion, he does not sow discord among his children. "God is not one who

likes things to be disorderly and upset. He likes harmony, and he finds it in all the other churches"
(1 Corinthians 14:33). "If you do this you will experience God's peace, which is far more wonderful than the human mind can understand. His peace will keep your thoughts and your hearts quiet and at rest as you trust in Christ Jesus" (Philippians 4:7). "Let the peace of heart which comes from Christ be always present in your hearts and lives, for this is your responsiblility and privilege as members of his body. And always be thankful" (Colossians 3:15). When we read about the quarrelsome heart in Proverbs, we feel we must examine our own hearts. The quarrelsome heart is at war with itself and with God. It is a heart that knows no peace.

A PRINCIPLE REVEALED

God's Word reveals a simple principle about the quarrelsome heart. "A quick-tempered man starts fights" (15:18). Such a man is at the mercy of his passions. He is set off at the snapping of a finger. Here is the basic principle: quarrels do not depend on issues, but on people. The particular issues do not matter. The real problem is in the heart. A man whose heart has a quarrel within it is easily involved in arguments and strife. Issues are never the real causes of strife.

It takes two to fight. That's true within us too. God will never fight with us unless we fight with him, unless we struggle against his will. We can have peace in our hearts only when we let the peace of God rule (Colossians 3:15). The peace of God will rule the hearts of his children unless they pull against him and break away from guidance. Then contention will fill their lives. When we obey God, we have peace. When we resist God, we lose that peace and strife results. We quarrel with God by turning against him, rebelling against him, and rejecting him. A quarrelsome heart is at war with God.

It does not really matter what the issue is in our hearts. It may be some flagrant sin that everyone knows about, or it may be a quiet, insidious thing known only to us and to God. The issue itself is insignificant. When we revolt against God, we are in rebellion against him and a quarrel comes into our hearts. The outward expression of our sin is not the key to our quarrelsome hearts. The problem is that our hearts have turned away from God, have violated his principles; we have rebelled against him and his peace.

A quarrelsome heart betrays the trust that God puts in it, betrays the Savior who brought our salvation to us, and betrays the trust of our friends. "Don't plot against your neighbor; he is trusting you" (3:29). If our hearts always think the worst, always look for the bad side, always try to find fault or delight in criticism, we constantly betray the trust of our friends and neighbors. There can then be no peace in our hearts.

A PRESENCE VIOLATED

The quarrelsome heart violates God's presence within it. If we are not at peace with God, we cannot be at peace with others. We are social beings. We were created for fellowship. We need it. If we interrupt the fellowship we have with others, strife tears us apart. We need to be at peace within in order to be at peace with others.

For every quarrel we see expressed or every misunderstanding we perceive, thousands exist in the form of resentment, bitterness, anger, and hatred that may never appear on the surface. Although they may never reveal themselves outwardly, they are there. We cannot give ourselves to others because we are not at peace. There is a strife and struggle within, and we are torn apart. A person with a quarrelsome heart is isolated by his fears. A quarrelsome heart cannot be loyal and concerned, because something eats at it and violates the fellowship that ought to exist between people.

A quarrelsome heart also violates the fellowship between God and man. "For there are six things the Lord hates—no seven: haughtiness, lying, murdering, plotting evil, eagerness to do wrong, a false witness, sowing discord among brothers" (6:16-19). Wherever there is dissonance or discord in the heart, whether it expresses itself or not, it is an abomination to God. God is the author of peace, and regardless of what others may do, he wants us to be at peace with him.

Quarrelsome hearts are also selfish. "Greed causes fighting; trusting God leads to prosperity" (28:25). A greedy heart will not bow to God. "Prosperity" in this text does not mean material wealth, but rather satisfaction, contentment, peace with self, God, and others. God never wants our hearts to be torn apart in rebellion against him. He wants us to have peace like a river in our hearts, peace in every circumstance, peace we can only have as we allow God to control our lives.

A PRIORITY ESTABLISHED

All the false teachings of the world tell us things we ought to do, but never tell us how to do them. Our God is not like that. He not only gives us directions for life, but he also tells us how we are to put them into action. "If you want favor with both God and man, and a reputation for good judgment and common sense, then trust the Lord completely; don't ever trust yourself. In everything you do, put God first, and he will direct you and crown your efforts with success" (3:4-6).

The priority is simple: trust in God. Just as Jesus multiplied the lunch of a lad to feed 5,000 men, women, and children, God will take the faith we bring to him and multiply it. He will make it more than adequate for our needs because he will invest his very being in us. As we trust the Lord instead of our own understanding, he will take contention and strife from our hearts and replace them with the peace that passes all understanding.

One of the most gracious persons in all the world was Dr. Kyle M. Yates of Baylor University. He had a special way about him. When asked about his gracious spirit one day, he replied, "Years ago I was a professor at Southern Seminary in Louisville, Kentucky. I had an early morning class, a large class. In that class sat a young man who came in on time every morning and slept through every class. For a while I watched that until one morning it finally got the best of me. I made an example of that young man. I woke him up abruptly and told him that if he were going to come to class, he should at least have the decency to be prepared and stay awake. After the class a student came up to me and said, 'Dr. Yates, the young man that you were so critical of today is struggling to stay in seminary. He works all night long and goes to classes all day. His wife is in the hospital, dying of cancer. He is doing the best he can. I wish you had not said what you did.' I had let my heart and mind get angry, and it exploded. I had done something I could never repair. I decided then that I would ask God to give me a sweet, kind heart every day and to take away any thought of condemnation or anything that might cause me to do such a thing again.''

We will generally find what we look for in life. If we want someone to be angry with, somebody will oblige us. If we look for something to criticize, we'll find it. There will always be something we can be unhappy about if we want to be. Likewise, if we look for God's peace and honestly recognize our own sins, our souls will have such a passion for God that we will not have time to merely protest the sins of others. We will be at peace.

Wrong attitudes come easily. It's easy to get angry or distressed. It's easy to have war in our souls. But we must be diligent if we are to know peace. "It is an honor for a man to stay out of a fight. Only fools insist on quarreling" (20:3). We are to stand aloof from quarrels and give attention to being the kind of persons we ought to be. God will do this in us through Jesus Christ.

"For Christ himself is our way of peace. He has made peace between us Jews and you Gentiles by making us all one family, breaking down the wall of contempt that used to separate us. By his death he ended the angry resentment between us, caused by the Jewish laws which favored the Jews and excluded the Gentiles, for he died to annul that whole system of Jewish laws. Then he took the two groups that had been opposed to each other and made them parts of himself; thus he fused us together to become one new person, and at last there was peace. As parts of the same body, our anger against each other has disappeared, for both of us have been reconciled to God" (Ephesians 2:14-16).

If we are bound by strife and contention with others, we can commit ourselves to Jesus Christ—he will give us peace.

The Truly Fulfilled Woman

A virtuous woman is a complete woman, a happy woman, a fulfilled woman. "If you can find a truly good wife, she is worth more than precious gems! Her husband can trust her, and she will richly satisfy his needs. She will not hinder him, but help him all her life" (31:10-12). This is one of the most beautiful descriptions of personhood to be found in all literature.

If we are to be fulfilled persons, we need to possess the characteristics of the virtuous woman. She seems to be the personification of all the virtues and strengths of character urged upon us throughout Proverbs. She is a model for all of us, whether men, women or children.

HER INCOMPARABLE VALUE
"If you can find a truly good wife, she is worth more than precious gems!" (31:10). A woman like that is worth more than we could pay. The truly fulfilled woman is of incomparable value because she complements her husband. "Her husband can trust her, and she will richly satisfy his needs. She will not hinder

him, but help him all her life" (31:11, 12). She will encourage her husband. She will uplift him and be his companion. She will support him. She buoys his spirit, lifts him up, and stands by his side.

Such a woman is cherished because she contributes to her husband's success. "She finds wool and flax and busily spins it. She buys imported foods, brought by ship from distant ports. She gets up before dawn to prepare breakfast for her household, and plans the day's work for her servant girls. She goes out to inspect a field, and buys it; with her own hands she plants a vineyard. She is energetic, a hard worker, and watches for bargains. She works far into the night! She sews for the poor, and generously gives to the needy. She has no fear of winter for the household, for she has made warm clothes for all of them. She also upholsters with finest tapestry; her own clothing is beautifully made—a purple gown of pure linen" (31:13-22). She works tirelessly to provide for her family's needs at home and enhances her husband's reputation—"her husband is well known, for he sits in the council chamber with the other civic leaders" (31:23). She is cherished by her husband because of her contribution to his life. Most of us must acknowledge that our successes in life have been very closely related to the encouragement and efforts of our wives as they stand by our sides.

HER CREATIVE ENERGY

 Just reading Proverbs 31:10-31 would tire most of us. Imagine what this woman accomplishes in a single day.

She improves everything around her—"she finds wool and flax and busily spins it" (31:13). A better translation of that is, "she shall never want for wool." She always makes new wool available.

She uses every moment and every opportunity to its fullest potential. She does not waste time. She is not lazy, choosing rather to be energetic, tireless. "She gets up before dawn to prepare breakfast for her household, and plans the day's work for her servant girls" (31:15). Not only that, "she works far into the night!" (31:18). A hard worker, she purchases a field, plants a vineyard, sells the crop, sews for her family. She lives life to its fullest and adequately prepares for the future—"She has no fear of winter for her household, for she has made warm clothes for all of them" (31:21). "She is a woman of strength and dignity, and has no fear of old age" (31:25). One translator renders this verse, "She shall laugh at the uncertainty of the future because she is ready for it." She is ready for her retirement years— she lives life at its best. She enriches every moment that God gives to her. She sees every moment as a shining opportunity. She greets each new day without fear.

HER COMPASSIONATE WISDOM

"She sews for the poor, and generously gives to the needy" (31:19, 20). This woman stays up late and gets up early in the morning. In addition to her household chores, she buys more land so she can cultivate it and have a bigger garden to tend. She is a busy woman, but she still has time for the poor and needy. She doesn't turn the beggar away. She loves to share what she has with others. She has a concern for other people. She blesses everyone with whom she comes in contact.

In contrast, none of us likes to be around a selfish person, one who doesn't care about anyone else.

When this woman opens her mouth, she speaks wisdom. Her children give attention to what she says. She is often sought out by friends and others around her because "when she speaks, her words are wise, and kindness is the rule for everything she says" (31:26). That passage could be translated, "Everything she does is governed by kindness." She is not abrasive—there is no wisdom in abrasiveness. She does not run roughshod over others—there is no wisdom in running roughshod over people. She is not unkind, unsympathetic, or unfeeling toward others. She is wise and wisdom says, "I care for you."

That is the truly fulfilled woman. She is a model for us because she is wise.

HER EXCELLENT PRAISE

Because she is of such great value, because her creative energy blesses all those around her, because her wisdom and compassion is known abroad, the virtuous woman is praised. "Her children stand and bless her; so does her husband. He praises her with these words: 'There are many fine women in the world, but you are the best of them all!' " (31:28, 29). Her name is synonymous with excellence. Surely her life is fulfilled for herself as well as others. As a result, she receives the fruit of her hands and her own works praise her.

Her praise is excellent because someone else is praising her. It is easy to praise ourselves and to give ourselves credit for our achievements. However, it is better for someone else to make an objective evaluation of our lives and work and to praise us for them. We are to live in such a way that our recognition will be based upon the fruit in our lives. "Praise her for the many fine things she does. These good deeds of hers shall bring her honor and recognition from even the leaders of the nations" (31:31).

Our lives are the basis for any praise or honor we receive. Our lives are not to be hidden in the shadows. We are to live openly, with honesty and integrity so people can see the work of Christ in us. Just as the works of the truly fulfilled woman reveal her character and indicate that her praise is deserved, so should ours. Just as God has used her to bless those around her, so he should be able to use us to bless those around us.

HER GENUINE BEAUTY

The truly fulfilled woman's genuine beauty is her most significant characteristic. "Charm can be deceptive and beauty doesn't last, but a woman who fears and reverences God shall be greatly praised" (31:30). Physical beauty and grace in themselves are empty, they don't last. The fulfilled woman "has no fear of old age" (31:25), when physical beauty is taken away. Time steals from us what we appear to be on the surface. Our physical attributes change; such beauty is only skin deep. Real beauty is what is within us, and it brings life and blessing to those around us.

If we want to be this kind of person, we must fear the Lord. A person whom people cherish, a person of incomparable value, a person whom people seek to have around is one who reverences God. If we want to use our creative energies as blessings to all, we must obey our Lord. If we would have wisdom and compassion, and deserved praise from others, we must walk with God. The secret of our success is our commitment to our Lord. We must be what he wants us to be. We are naturally rude, thoughtless, sinful, selfish. We can be turned to anger and hatred easily. We cannot be wise or fruitful if God is not in control of our lives. It all begins with the fear of the Lord. When we come to God in reverence, trust and obedience, he gives to us the basis for forming a life that can have all of these characteristics of the truly fulfilled woman.

The beautiful description of the life of the truly fulfilled woman here in Proverbs 31 is a challenge to all women, indeed to all mankind. Only through God's help can we become truly complete persons.

The
Reality
of God

Some writers say the book of Proverbs has no real notion of God, that its concept of God is rather primitive. Actually, God is no afterthought or incidental truth in Proverbs. He is at the very heart of the book. He is shown to be the creator and controller who puts everything in its place and keeps it there.

Proverbs teaches that there are no loose ends with God, no accidents, because he is in control, he is involved. Every created thing fits into the pattern of this world because of him. In his providence and wisdom, he designed it, created it, and sustains it. "We can make our plans, but the final outcome is in God's hands. We can always 'prove' that we are right, but is the Lord convinced? Commit your work to the Lord, then it will succeed. The Lord has made everything for his own purposes—even the wicked, for punishment" (16:1-4).

In Proverbs the Holy Spirit reveals three things to us about the reality of God.

AWARENESS OF SIN

Throughout Proverbs there is a keen awareness of sin, and of the holiness of God. If we have a concept of evil, we have a concept of a God whose holiness is offended by sin. The first thing that tells us that the writer of Proverbs had a deep sense of the presence of God is his deep awareness of his own sin—"Iniquity is atoned for by mercy and truth; evil is avoided by reverence for God" (16:6).

"Who can ever say, 'I have cleansed my heart; I am sinless'?" (20:9). No man can say he has made his own heart clean and that he is free from sin. "For God, who knows all hearts, knows yours, and he knows you knew! And he will reward everyone according to his deeds" (24:12). We try to hide something from God, we try to say there is no sin in our lives, but God is aware of our sins and we are accountable for them. "A man who refuses to admit his mistakes can never be successful. But if he confesses and forsakes them, he gets another chance" (28:13).

Because the holy God is no afterthought, no footnote, but is rather at the very center of life, we need to heed his words.

Wherever there is an awareness of failure, frustration, defeat, and sin, there is also a deepseated awareness that there is a God to whom we are responsible. Sin without forgiveness and cleansing brings guilt and despair, guilt that keeps us aware of our spiritual bankruptcy before God.

AWARENESS OF A PERSONAL GOD

The book of Proverbs also teaches us about the awareness of a *personal* God. "These girls have abandoned
their husbands and flouted the laws of God" (2:17). The
translated word "God" is the Hebrew word for Jehovah
or Yahweh, the proper, personal name for God. "For if I
grow rich, I may become content without God. And if I
am too poor, I may steal, and thus insult God's holy
name" (30:9). There it is again. Jehovah, Yahweh, Lord,
God—these all are personal names of a personal God.
He is my God, your God, a personal God with whom
we have to do.

This personal God is interested in us individually.
He is not passively waiting for us to stumble around
and perhaps find him. He is seeking us, searching for
us. In the first chapter of Proverbs, the word "wisdom"
is used with God. "Wisdom shouts in the streets for a
hearing. She calls out to the crowds along Main Street,
and to the judges in their courts, and to everyone in all
the land: 'You simpletons!' she cries. 'How long will
you go on being fools? How long will you scoff at wisdom and fight the facts? Come here and listen to me! I'll
pour out the spirit of wisdom upon you, and make you
wise' " (1:20-23). God is interested in us.

The picture of God in Proverbs is the same as that
seen in the New Testament, where God is pictured as a
loving Father searching for his children. God is concerned about his creation. He didn't wait for us to clean
up our lives, or to decide we wanted him to help us.
God took the initiative and sent Jesus Christ into the
world to save us. God seeking man—that's the God of

Proverbs and of the New Testament. Ours is a God who seeks the hearts of men. If he did not seek us, we could not be saved. He draws us to himself. Our God is a personal God who seeks a personal response from us.

In addition, Proverbs tell us that God is a covenant maker. Not only does God seek men, he does it so intently that he makes an agreement, a covenant with them. He makes certain guarantees to his children. The word "God" appears about one hundred times in Proverbs in the English Bible. Most of these occurrences use the covenant name for God, Yahweh, Jehovah, Lord. That is the name God used with Abraham and with Moses. It represents a God who loves his people, who is personally concerned about them. It shows a God who said, "I am going to send a Redeemer to you." This personal God is the covenant God, the God who keeps his word, the God who will never turn his back on us. He is the God we can trust completely. He takes care of his people.

God is also a self-disclosing God. He tells us about himself. He does not leave it to us to presume about him in nature. He sent his Son so that we might know what he was like. He sent his Spirit to move in the lives of holy men and record for us his words. He revealed himself to us. "For the Lord grants wisdom! His every word is a treasure of knowledge and understanding" (2:6). God wants us to know him.

A CONTEMPORARY GOD

God is forever present. He is our personal God and he is the covenant God who seeks man. These certainly go together. Still, our God is not a God of the past, he is not buried in antiquity. He is a God of the present, a God of the now. He is a God who knows our needs. Everything he did back then is just an encouragement to let us know what he can do for us now. He is forever contemporary to his children.

"Trust the Lord completely; don't ever trust yourself" (3:5). That unconditional promise is as real today as it ever has been in the past. Our personal, covenant, and contemporary God is alive and active. He still speaks to our hearts. He still deals with our needs. He still shares our grief. He still gives wisdom for our perplexities. He still gives us clear vision for the future. He works in our lives now as he did back then. We can trust him with all our hearts. "In everything you do, put God first, and he will direct you and crown your efforts with success" (3:6). That is a beautiful promise from God himself. He is a God who is "the same yesterday, today, and forever" (Hebrews 13:8). That's why he can say, "I will never, *never* fail you nor forsake you" (Hebrews 13:5).

Through the ages God's children have trusted him, and he directed them. As a result, we can believe what he tells us now and can share that truth with others. The Lord is our defender (22:19-23). If our hearts are heavy, if we are oppressed, if we face discouragement, we can trust God. When we have been brought face to face with an experience that threatens our peace of heart and our tranquility of soul, we can turn to God. He will plead our cause. He will direct our paths. He is a God for today. Whatever our needs may be, we can turn to him and he will protect us. He is our covenant-keeping God. He is omnipotent (all-powerful), omnipresent (all-present), omniscient (all-knowing), and eternal.

If we share God's Word, if we believe it, if we base our lives upon it, God will confirm to us that he is real. He will prove to us that he is not just a God of the past. He is a God of the here and now. He is the God of Proverbs. He has acted in the past and today stands ready to comfort broken hearts, piece together broken dreams, redirect shattered lives, and banish sin. The fear of him is the beginning of wisdom. He is the alpha and the omega, the first and the last.

"Trust the Lord completely; don't ever trust yourself. In everything you do, put God first, and he will direct you and crown your efforts with success" (3:5, 6). God's promise to us means nothing unless we respond to him, something we must do for ourselves. God will never force us to confess that he is Lord. We have the capacity to say "yes" or "no" to God. We can know him, and so know forgiveness. He is the God of Proverbs, and he seeks to be our God too.